The Coffee Break Guide to Business Plans for Writers

THE STEP-BY-STEP GUIDE TO TAKING CONTROL OF YOUR WRITING CAREER

Amy Denim

Coffee Break Publishing
DENVER, COLORADO

Coffee Break Publishing
www.coffeebreaksocialmedia.com

Book Layout ©2013 BookDesignTemplates.com

ISBN-13:978-0615946856
ISBN-10:0615946852

The Coffee Break Guide to Business Plans for Writers: The Step-by-Step Guide to Taking Control of Your Writing Career/ Amy Denim.—1st ed.

Contents

Take Control of Your Career 11

Yes, You are a Business 15

Publishing Routes... 27

Every Author.. 33

The Coffee Break Business Plan.. 37

Goals.. 41

What to Include in Your Business Plan............................. 59

Time to Write Your Plan.. 67

The Blurb 69

The Cover 74

Acknowledgements Page.. 80

The Chapters 82

Shelves 89

Get in the Bag... 96

The Bank.. 102

Book by book 112

Tracking and evaluating your business plan.................... 118

See, You Can Do This i

Resources.. i

The Coffee Break Guide to Social Media for Writers:.... vii

A Thank You From the Author.. xx

Dedication

For Katie,

*who helps me remember everyday
why I write.*

Love you.

Acknowledgements

This book would not have been possible without some amazing people in my life who believed in me and the ideas floating around in my head and my laptop.

Special thanks to my Beta reader Heather Lire. You better have your business plan finished now.

I can't thank Diane Whiddon at Novel Website Design enough for designing CoffeeBreakSocialMedia.com and especially for her insights into being an entrepreneur.

Big thanks to Danica Favorite and Jon Tandler for putting the idea that every author should absolutely have a business plan into my head in the first place. If I hadn't attended your workshops I'd still be flailing about.

Pictures are worth a thousand words, so here's a thousand thanks to Mike Sands at 3M&H Design for all his graphics help with covers and Facebook and websites, oh my!

A great big thank you to my editors Shannnon Janeczek and Ahuva Rogers. They are grammar and punctuation royalty, so any mistakes remaining in this book soooooo belong to me.

Take Control of Your Career

When I first started searching for information about writing a business plan, all I found were very formal plans designed for start-up businesses that offered services or products for sale, like sandwiches or cars.

A long and tedious report about my author life didn't appeal to me, but I wanted something more than just to set goals. So I took the formal titles and statements of a traditional business plan, converted them to accommodate the kind of work I planned to do as a writer, and created the plot for my work life. This is what you'll find in this book along with step-by-step instructions on how to create your own author business plan.

I've broken up the plan into sections and the idea is for you to work through them in the span of a coffee break. It can be overwhelming to sit down and write a great big business plan, but taking fifteen minutes to think about some of your goals is completely doable. Some sections will take longer than just one coffee break. Break those up into manageable tasks that you can do in fifteen to thirty minutes.

I'll ask you to consider your goals, think about the way you plan to publish, and where you are in the publishing journey. In each step, I provide ideas and questions you might want to consider for those varying goals. I decided to include them all together so that authors at all phases of publishing might benefit from other perspectives. You might just update and add to your goals by checking out ideas for traditional, self-published, or hybrid authors. Newbie authors can look at ideas for multi-book published authors to help plan their futures, and authors who've been publishing for years might get a new perspective on how to get the "woo-hoo" back in their business.

Additionally, you can write a plan for each book — if you really want to go crazy. I've provided considerations and a generic template to do just that.

Once you have a good idea of what to include in your business goals, you might also benefit from running the numbers. It can be hard to figure out how much money you'll actually make at writing, so doing a budget and some projections can help give you a realistic idea.

Throughout the book, I've provided links to downloadable documents. If you're reading the e-book, you can click on the links. If you're reading the print version, all of the links are on the resources page at the end of the book and on my website at

www.coffeebreaksocialmedia.com/books/resources.

Remember that a business plan is just that: a plan. It should be a living document that you can change as needed, but that should also keep you accountable to yourself and your business. It's also your life and your work. Not mine, not your father's—yours. You have to decide how much time, effort, and thought you are willing to put into it. You also get to choose what you want or need to include. This will vary drastically from person to person, and author to author.

Finally, if you've done all this work to put a plan together, you might want to measure how well you're achieving your goals along the way. The final chapters have ideas on how to do that and (for all you English majors out there) information on budgets, with a downloadable Excel spreadsheet template. It's not that scary, I promise. So go to it. Make your business plan.

Right now. Go.

CHAPTER 1

Yes, You are a Business

The Business of Being a Writer

Writers write. But in the new age of publishing (that's now) writers have to do a whole lot more than write. They have to establish a platform, market, engage on social media, attend conferences and readers' events, and more. If a writer decides they want to self-publish, they also have to create or contract the cover art, find an independent editor, research the market, and stay on top of technological updates. Being a writer is no easy business.

That's right. It's a business. The second you decided to get your work published, be it by a traditional publisher or on your own, you became a business. Most of us don't think of our writing efforts in that way. We just write. Right?

I am not an accountant (or a lawyer). I am a writer. One who has spent years studying the business of writing. Yes, we all take classes on craft, do research for our books, and have maybe even thought about a marketing plan. We put a whole lot of effort into our books, so why not put that same effort into yourself? You are, after all, your business's greatest asset. Without you, there is no business.

Unless this is a hobby and the only people who are ever going to read your work are your family and pets, then you absolutely are a business. And if you're going to be a business, then you're going to want a business plan.

A lot of writers are very right-brained creative people to whom spreadsheets and rows of numbers are like a bad itching powder in their pants. (There are plenty of exceptions to that generalization. Accountants who write romance, for example.) This book has information that you just might want a spreadsheet for, but there is also plenty of creative thinking and fluffy rainbows in designing your work life. We are, after all, creating your dream here.

If you are a plotter, you're going to love creating a business plan It will be just like plotting your action/ adventure/ thriller/ romance/ fantasy novel, but better because it's your real life you'll be planning. If you're a pantser, I've got plenty for you to do, too. Yes, I am going to make you think about your happily ever after and the steps to take to get there — but don't worry, you can change it anytime you like.

Why Do I Need a Business Plan?

"Writing isn't a business that requires investors or small business loans. What good does a business plan do me?"

You're correct. Writing is not your typical small start-up that requires you to write a proposal with tables and charts to present to your bank or venture capitalists, so you can get money for your project. (Although some authors do raise funds to support their writing efforts.) The best way a plan can help you is by organizing your goals for your writing career, understanding the industry you'll be working in, and managing your writing efforts toward success.

"I'm not making any money being a writer. Why do I need a business plan?"

Well, I'm glad you asked. First, I hope you plan to make some money for all your hard work. You deserve to. Don't get me wrong, you're not likely going to make a katrillion dollars (some people do, though), but there are plenty of people out there making a decent living from writing. So think positively and plan for it.

"But it takes years to get published. Why do I need a business plan now, why not wait until I sell a book?"

Really? Do you think successful businesses build their plans after they sell their first product? No way. They planned and worked and toiled to make sure that product was the best they could make it, and then sent it out into the world, hoping someone would produce it. Some decided to produce it themselves and then marketed the heck out of their product, making all their friends and family members buy it. Sound familiar? It should. That's exactly what writers do. And those businesses had a good solid plan to make that happen.

Taxes

First of all, I am not an accountant or an attorney, so this does not constitute legal or financial advice. Don't sue me. Just be sure to check with a financial advisor when making your tax and other financial decisions. It can be hard for writers to have conversations about taxes and I think we should start a dialogue about it. So, here goes.

The three most feared letters in America are (no, not the CIA, FBI, or NRA) I, R, and S. Death and taxes, baby. Both are big, dark, and frightening unknowns. As a self-employed writer there is no faceless company to take care of your income tax, 401(k) or social security. (And if you're outside the US of A, I'm sure your tax and regulatory government agency is just as scary as ours.)

If you are lucky enough to be making some money from your writing ventures, have you paid Uncle Sam his share? No?

Uh-oh.

Taxes. Another really good reason to have a business plan.

The only time we all really fear the taxman is when he sends you the letter that says you're being audited. The one and only way to win the audit game? Documentation. A business plan is all kinds of good documentation. Your auditor will be happy as a clam to see one in the file (read: shoebox) where you keep your receipts.

The first thing to do is determine whether your writing is a business or a hobby. Here are some questions to answer for yourself:

Does the time and effort put into the activity indicate an intention to make a profit?

How do you know, or how can you prove, that your writing activities indicate an intention to make a profit?

Here are a couple of ways. Keep a log of your time spent writing, or how many words you write a day. There are a number of websites, apps, and software to help track your time. Google it and you'll find a plethora. Same goes for tracking word count. You can use a simple spreadsheet or even a paper logbook to track your time and effort. Just as long as you are consistent. Keep a copy of your logged hours or word counts for that taxman.

Now take a good look at the time you spend on the words you get written in the next month, week, and year. You are your own employee for this business; would you hire you? Would you fire yourself for your time and effort spent?

What else are you doing to try and make a profit? How do authors make money? The first thing that comes to mind is by selling books. If you are going the traditional publishing route, there are some gatekeepers, like agents and editors. You can show your intention to make a profit by having documentation that you have contacted them. Have you sent out query letters? Keep track of who and when you sent them, and any replies you've received. If you're self-publishing, keep your documentation on setting up accounts with the publishing platforms, i.e. your CreateSpace, Smashwords, or other account information. Or if you've actually pushed the publish button, you can certainly provide information on the sales of your books.

There are handy dandy downloadable Excel tools to track everything from wordcount to sales rankings at my website www.CoffeeBreakSocialMedia.com/Books/Resources.

You know how else you can show your time and effort put into writing? Your business plan. Make it, use it, love it, ward off the IRS auditor with it.

Does the taxpayer depend on income from the activity?

Well, do you? Have you quit your job to write full-time? That totally counts. Even if you've reduced your hours. This one is a lot easier to prove if you're already making some money from writing. Check out your percentage of income from writing as compared to the total. Now evaluate. Could you live at your current level without that money?

If there are losses, are they due to circumstances beyond the taxpayer's control, or did they occur in the start-up phase of the business?

Writers can not control the whims of agents and editors. If they like your book, are having a good hair day, and haven't acquired something similar that day, week, month or year, then maybe, just maybe they'll take you on. But how do you prove that? Again, go back to your query letters.

If you don't feel like that's enough, hit the blogs. There are tons of stories out there from both sides of the acquisition table that talk about how hard it is to break into this business. Keep some of those on file.

Self-publishing folks can use those blogs, too. There are a whole lot of review sites that still don't read self-published work. Use it to your advantage for once. Make a list of review sites that say they don't review self-published books. Also keep track of who you've requested reviews from, when you submitted, whether they accepted your book or not, when they reviewed it (if they did), and what kind of a review you received. Same goes for other places that have reviews like Amazon, Goodreads, and others. Also, take a screen shot of your Amazon ranking, or if you have access, download the information from your Amazon author page. If that isn't proof that you are not in control, I don't know what is.

Published authors can ask their publisher for a copy of their book's marketing schedule. Oh, don't have one? Proof perfect, right there. Do have one? Unless you're Nora Roberts and your publisher just spent a billion dollars in co-op money on your book, once again, you've got pretty darn good proof that some circumstances are beyond your control.

Does start-up phase mean the 1,000 years we all write before getting published? Or does that also count the whole time you are a debut author? How about up until you earn out your advance?

Has the taxpayer changed methods of operation to improve profitability?

Have you taken any craft classes and applied your learnings to your writing? Good job. You've changed your method of operation. Have you written in a new genre? Have you joined a critique group or gotten a critique partner? How about beta readers? Enter a new contest? These are all great changes to your methods of operation.

Have you started blogging? Did you spend time and money on new marketing efforts? Did you do your first ever book signing, or appear at a new bookstore, writers' event, or conference? Great work. These are all more changes to your methods.

Have you gone from traditional publishing to self-publishing? How about from a digital first press to print, or even switched publishers or publish with a new group? Vice versa? Those are some serious changes to improve your profitability.

This blueprint you're putting together can help you look to the future for when and where it's time to make some changes to your method of operations. Those goals you've set out in your plan. Each one of those is a proposed change. Booyah!

Does the taxpayer or his/her advisors have the knowledge needed to carry on the activity as a successful business?

If you've gotten an agent, editor, literary attorney, or an accountant who has worked with authors and writers before, then you have advisors that have the knowledge. Do you belong to a national writers' organization like Romance Writers of America, Sisters in Crime, Science Fiction and Fantasy Writers of America, American Society of Journalists and Authors, Society of Children's Book Writers and Illustrators, a local writers' group, or a plethora of others? That's a great step in the right direction toward getting the information you need about being a successful writer.

Have you attended workshops, discussions, made friends with other writers, read up on your craft or books dealing with the business of writing (like this one), or written a book yourself? Well then you've got the knowledge.

Has the taxpayer made a profit in similar activities in the past?

This doesn't have to mean making a profit from the same kind of writing you're doing right now. Have you ever had a job where you had to write something? A report, a business letter, a technical manual? Well then you've made a profit from a similar activity, haven't you?

Does the activity make a profit in some years?

Publishing is a fickle business, and if you're publishing traditionally it can be years between book releases. Some years you'll make a profit and other years you won't. Keep a copy of those royalty statements!

Can the taxpayer expect to make a profit in the future from the appreciation of assets used in the activity?

What are your writing business assets? Yes, it's your brain, your imagination, and your fingers. But those don't count. Your laptop probably doesn't either, unless you use it exclusively for your writing business. But you know what does? Your words. Yep, all those manuscripts you've shoved under the bed. Assets. Once you're actually published, those books are most definitely your assets. Do you expect to make a profit in the future from those books? (You better have said yes.)

Here's another place where your preparations are going to come in handy. How do you prove you expect to make a profit? Well, it's right there on page whatever of your business plan. When, where, and how you expect to make a profit. Possibly even how much.

You don't have to be able to answer yes to each of these questions for your writing to qualify as a business instead of a hobby. You only need to answer yes to about half or so. If you can't answer yes to four of them, can you change some of the ways you operate in order to be able to say yes?

Remember, I'm not an accountant, nor am I a representative of the IRS. I did get these questions off their website, though. The best thing you can do for your business is to hire an accountant (smartest business decision I ever made). And make sure you get one familiar with the business of being a writer, not just your Uncle Joe who works for Jackson Hewitt two months out of the year. A good accountant will help you figure out if you really are a business or a hobby, and more importantly, what you can write off, legally.

Yes, you will have to keep your receipts for EVERYTHING, and not in a shoebox. They have to be all organized and pretty. Your accountant can help you figure out which receipts to actually hold on to and what categories to put them into. Once again, this is all documentation to ward off the dreaded audit. If you have a budget and you keep track of those expenses on that budget, well that's just more documentation to show your cute, but nerdy IRS agent.

Legal Entities

A quick note on your choice of legal entity. You are a business and therefore you are also a legal entity. But there are several choices on what kind of entity you can be. The best way to figure out what kind to choose is by talking to your accountant and a lawyer. The following is not legal or tax advice, but general information to get you started.

If you are just starting out as a writer, either pre-published or having one or two books released and available for sale, you probably want to stick with being a sole proprietor. You already are that now. The biggest advantage of a sole proprietorship is that you can file your author business taxes on a Schedule C of your regular 1040 tax return for US tax filers. If you have an accountant helping you with your taxes, it shouldn't cost anything or very much more than you are already paying.

If you choose to stick with sole proprietorship, and especially if you are self-publishing, you may want to file a trade name or Doing Business As, commonly known as a DBA. The advantage of a trade name/DBA for authors is that it can make things organizationally separate.

If you are self-publishing and want to file under your publishing entity name that is not just your own name, you'll need to file a trade name/DBA. In some states your DBA will be good statewide and in others, just in your county. There are usually small fees associated with filing and the information must be renewed periodically. You should be able to find the information on your state's website, or if all else fails, Google.

The next choice that is common for many authors, especially once they are multi-published, is a Limited Liability Company, commonly seen as LLC. This requires formal legal organization and is intended to do exactly what the name says, provide limited liability to its members. You will have to form an LLC through your state, which will include paperwork including Articles of Organization, federal and regulatory filings, and an Operating Agreement. It can cost anywhere from $75 to $800 (depending on your state) for extra accounting and registration. It also adds a Schedule C to your tax returns. Most states have information on their websites. And there are tons of websites and lawyers that can help you through the process, for a fee.

Then there are Corporations. These are for the authors who've been publishing for multiple years, are multi-published, and also likely multi-millionaires. Corporations are formed under state law and require documentation such as Articles, Bylaws, minutes, share certificates, tax and regulatory filings, and possibly buy/sell agreements.

"C" Corporations are taxed at the corporate level and Subchapter "S" Corporations' owners are taxed in proportion to ownership. "S" corporations also have to satisfy certain requirements under the Internal Revenue Code. You will likely need a lawyer to form a corporation.

If you are choosing the path of traditional publishing you should know that most traditional publishers don't allow contracts to be signed by an entity, and even if they do, you will probably still have to personally guarantee the contract. If you form a company or corporation, you will register a copyright under your personal name/pen name. A limited liability does help separate your business assets from your personal assets, but because you're the owner of that company or corporation, your ass and your assets would still be on the line should you get sued.

Choosing your legal entity is a big decision and one best made with professional help.

CHAPTER 2

Publishing Routes

Choosing Your Path

Before we can delve very far into developing your business plan, we need a short discussion on the different paths to publishing in today's world. By the time this book is published, there will probably be new and exciting ways to get a book published. It's been said by many that this is the era of the author.

For thousands of years, publishing has been a career route for a select few. With each new reinvention of the business, from the printing press to Amazon, the possibility of becoming a published author opens up to more and more people. Today, anyone who has access to a computer can become a published author in less than a day if they want to.

If you're reading this book, you've chosen to make publishing your business. Congratulations. But just because you've decided to become a published author doesn't mean you know how to do it, or even the best path to publishing for you. Some of you might even know there is more than one choice.

Here are some of the basics of becoming a published author these days.

The route to traditional publishing

1. Write a book.
2. Query agents and editors.
3. Wait for months to hear any news.
4. Get rejected by agents and editors.
5. Rewrite your book.
6. Query more agents and editors.
7. Repeat steps one through five until you are accepted by an agent or editor.
8. Agent works with you to polish your manuscript.
9. Rewrite your book again.
10. Agent is happy with your work and begins to submit to traditional publishing houses.
11. Wait for months to hear any news while writing the next book.
12. Get rejected by editors.
13. Rewrite your book.
14. Your agent submits to new editors.
15. Wait for months to hear any news while you write the next book.
16. Repeat steps 8–15 until an editor accepts your book.
17. Editor presents your book to the acquisitions committee or the publisher.
18. Acquisitions committee or the publisher declines to purchase your book.
19. Repeat steps 8–18 until a publisher buys your book.
20. Cel-e-brate good times, come on!
21. Wait months for a contract while you write the next book.

22. Wait months for the first third of your advance while you write the next book.
23. Wait months for edits from your editor while you write the next book.
24. Write frantically to get your edits back to the editor within two weeks so your book can still be published on schedule.
25. You're asked what your marketing plan is and get a phone call with an in-house PR person.
26. You're asked to submit information about what you'd like to see on your cover.
27. Get to see the title of your book and what your cover looks like.
28. Get copy edits and have 48 hours to return them with any error corrections.
29. Get an uncorrected Advanced Reader's Copy of your book and the last chance to make any corrections to typos only.
30. Get the next third of your advance.
31. Get a firm-ish release date.
32. Get a publicity schedule from the in-house PR, which may include a blog tour.
33. The sales team adds your book to the catalog.
34. Your book goes on pre-sale.
35. Market your ass off.
36. It's release day! Yay!
37. Get the final third of your advance (unless you sold a series or signed a multi-book contract and then wait until you've turned in and/or had the first three books printed).

38. Receive your first royalty statement for the first three months of sales (six months ago) nine months later. The royalty statement makes no sense.

39. You call your agent who helps explain your royalty statement and shows you that you've had 60 percent returns.

40. Earn out your advance and start earning actual royalties on your book three years later.

41. Write the next book.

The route to self-publishing

1. Write a book.

2. Possibly start down the traditional publishing path, decide it is outdated and not worth your time and effort.

3. Decide to self-publish your book.

4. Have your book professionally edited.

5. Revise your book based on content edits.

6. Have your book copy edited.

7. Make suggested changes from your copy editor.

8. Have your book proofread.

9. Fix any remaining errors (although inevitably there will still be some).

10. Hire a cover artist and work with them to get the best cover you can.

11. Have your book formatted for each platform you intend to publish on (e-books, print etc.).

12. Create and begin executing a marketing plan.

13. Three months later, publish your book on various platforms (which is 42 steps in and of itself) while you write the next book.
14. Watch your sales numbers like a hawk... while you write the next book.
15. One to two months later, get your first royalty payment.
16. Change your cover, back matter, and/or blurb to try to increase interest in your book.
17. Watch your sales like a hawk... while you write the next book.
18. Do more marketing efforts to increase sales and rankings... while you write the next book.
19. Do sales or other promotions to increase sales and rankings... while you write the next book.
20. Get your next royalty payment one month later.
21. Repeat steps 14–19.
22. Write the next book.

The hybrid author is someone who does a combination of the two types of publishing. Many authors may start out publishing traditionally and supplement with self-published works. If you are traditionally published, you'll have to check your contracts closely to see what you are allowed to self-publish later. You may want to start with a novella, or perhaps you've gotten the rights back to previously traditionally published titles. These are both great places to start a hybrid author career.

Only you can decide which is the right path to becoming a published author. You might try one and then try another, change your mind, and spend years struggling with your decision. But putting together a business plan can help you spend less time trying to figure out which path to follow and more time actually living your dreams.

CHAPTER 3

Every Author

Every Author's Business Plan

S tart with the basics, which every author can include:
Your writing/books.

In chapter five, we'll work on your goals, but start thinking about these questions. How many books are you planning to write this year? When are you going to write them? Can you create a production schedule? Remember, this is a plan. You can adjust it as you go if you end up writing more than expected, or if you can't hold to your own schedule. But hold yourself accountable. Really work to keep to those deadlines and be strict about giving yourself extensions. Check out more information for the different routes to publishing in your chosen path.

Money, Money, Money

How much money can you potentially make? I don't know. It all depends on you and how much effort you put into this business. Plus, it's not like you can Google "author salaries" to get any real numbers, since authors don't actually get a salary unless you're working for someone else. (In which case, I hope your employer has a good business plan.) Authors make everything from popcorn to Mega Powerball winnings. Most of them are somewhere in between.

You should include projections from book sales, like advances, royalties, and sale of rights (like foreign rights, movie rights, etc.). Even independent/self-published authors can sell those rights, particularly if their books are selling well.

Alternative and Passive Income Streams

Don't forget to include money you could be making from other income streams. (Oh, yes. Authors can make money from more things than just writing, and if you haven't considered them, here's a little primer.)

You know how to write, right? Consider some freelance writing. This includes magazines, newsletters, copy, technical writing, websites, and more.

Blogging is a great way to help establish your platform. "Monetizing a blog" means that you have ads on your website. I don't recommend monetizing your author website or blog, but you might consider blogging somewhere you can monetize. Maybe a review site, for books or other products.

Want to spend your writing time concentrating on your work instead of an additional income stream?

You've been studying and learning all about the publishing industry. Do you know how to do something that other authors need help with? This could be creating book covers, making a website, setting up blog tours, social media, book trailers, creating audio books, help with the craft, or anything else authors need or do.

Use that knowledge. Share it by teaching workshops. This will help you establish your platform, build credibility, and create additional income. Local writers' organizations are always looking for new speakers for their meetings. A one- or two-hour workshop can earn you anything from $25–$200 and up.

There are a lot of websites for authors that offer online workshops too. Don't even leave the comfort of your pajamas.

Start another part of your business by offering your expertise to other writers. Don't just teach them, do for them. I personally do not have the skills to design my own book covers, nor do I have the desire to learn how. If I need a professional book cover, I have to pay someone to do it for me. Could that person be you?

If you're a fiction writer with some expertise that other authors will find useful, write a non-fiction book about it.

Do you have books published? Are they for sale on Amazon? Consider being an Amazon affiliate. You absolutely have your books on your website (right?), and you have links to booksellers there too, so why not get paid for directing people to Amazon to buy your book?

Do you have a wildly popular series? Or just some really cool characters or lines in your book? Think about merchandise. A really easy way to sell merchandise that relates to your books is through a site like

Zazzle or Cafepress. You give them designs and they'll put it all over t-shirts, bags, key chains, and all kinds of other cool stuff your fans can buy.

CHAPTER 4

The Coffee Break Business Plan

Goals are an Important Part of a Business Plan

Whatever kind of writing you do, and no matter where you are on the path(s) to publishing you have chosen, the best and easiest place to start your plan is with some basic goals. Taking the time to think about what you truly want to do and accomplish with your writing will not only help you put together your strategy, but it will help you focus on actually getting your writing done.

Writers tend to be creative type people by nature, and often we get ideas for our writing from millions of places: dreams, TV shows, newspaper articles, books, real life. And when we get these ideas, we are excited about them. We want to write these stories down while they are fresh in our heads. So many authors get caught in a trap doing just that. They have half a dozen manuscripts started, and not a single one finished. You can't sell a book that isn't finished. Sure, you might get an advance on a proposal, but if you don't finish writing it, guess what? You have to give all that pretty money back.

By getting yourself straight on your goals, you can see where you need to concentrate your efforts. If you don't go all ADHD — look, a squirrel! — in your writing, you can get so much accomplished.

If all you ever do on your business plan is set some goals, well then you're far ahead of most other authors. If you don't finish reading the rest of this book and only write down some of your goals, I'll be a happy camper. But determining your goals is only the beginning, so do keep reading.

The Coffee Break Business Plan

Okay, put your thinking cap/top hat/beanie with the helicopter rotor /tiara on. It's time to think about what you really want.

The answers to these questions will become the basis of your entire plan. These questions are to get you started thinking about your goals, but don't go crazy here and spend hours making lists and/or daydreaming about your success as a writer.

I call this the Coffee break Business Plan. Chapter 5 is all about basic goals, so spend only a few minutes thinking about each of these questions. Write a couple of sentences to answer them or make yourself a nice bullet-point list. If you'd like a template to print out to help you with this exercise, you can download one at

www.coffeebreaksocialmedia.com/Books/Resources.

Grab a Cup of Coffee and a Pen

Write down the answers to these questions.

- How many books do you plan to write? In what genre?
- What's your projected word count?
- When will you finish each project? Or, how much time will you need to complete each project? (Don't forget to build in time for critiques, beta readers, editing, and all those other activities... besides actually writing the book.)
- How will you publish these books? Traditionally, self-published, a hybrid approach?
- If you're self-publishing, what services will you need and how much will you spend on those?
- Who is your competition? Who else writes books like yours?
- How will you sell and market your books?
- How much money will it cost you to publish and market? What services might you pay for to help you do that?
- How much money do you plan to make, and when will you see that revenue?
- When do you plan to achieve these goals?

There you go. You just created a business plan. For real. Laminate that sucker and put it up big and pretty in front of your computer. Every time you sit down to write, take a look and focus on writing to achieve those goals. If the IRS comes knocking, you can wave it in their faces

CHAPTER 5

Goals

Think Big

Have you ever read The Secret? It's a great little book all about the power of positive thinking. If you haven't read it, pick up a copy or watch it on Netflix. That's where I first discovered it.

One of the things I remember very specifically from the show is about a man who created vision boards. He cut out pictures from magazines of what he wanted his future to look like and pasted them onto bulletin boards. He had one for family, home, career, and more. He hung those boards in his office. Years later when he and his family were moving into the multi–million-dollar home they renovated, he took out those vision boards and realized they'd just moved into the same house he'd pinned on one of his boards years earlier. Not just a house that was similar—the exact house. This is the power of creating goals and then actually believing you will achieve them. Keep that in mind as you think about and create your goals in this chapter.

Start your goals setting by thinking big. When you first imagined being an author, what did that look like? Did you dream of the cabin in the mountains, sitting behind a desk with a gorgeous view inspiring you? How about being whisked away by your publisher in a private jet to your international multi-city book tour? Maybe you hoped someday to be sitting in a romantic restaurant with your sweetie trying to have a quiet dinner, only to be accosted by raving fans wanting you to sign their book, their t-shirt, their chest, or more.

Well, unless you're Nora Roberts, Steven King, or Richard Castle, this is unlikely to be what your life as a writer is like. And I don't think even they get the whole private jet thing. But that doesn't mean these can't be your goals. Think big, think positive, and work your way to being the rock-star author. It will take many years of hard work to get there, but if that's what you truly want, go for it. Think big, be big.

Think Realistic

Now that we have your big dream goals in mind, let's narrow that down to something realistic. What would make you happy or feel accomplished as a writer? Would you like to make enough money to live on, buy a house, buy a new car, take a vacation, pay your utility bills, or buy dinner? Maybe it's all of the above.

Or would you feel accomplished when you see your books on the shelf at the local brick-and-mortar books store? Maybe you want 100,000 followers for your blog, or to see your story up on the big screen. You decide. What would make you feel like you'd made it in the world of writing? When can you say to yourself (and maybe even others) "Yeah, I'm a writer"?

The Why Behind It All

Once you have some big and realistic goals, think about why you've chosen them. Is it just what everyone else expects of you or of a writer, or is it what you really want? Be really honest with yourself. Do you write because you love it, or because you have to? Are you in it for the money (I hope not), or because you yearn to share the innards of your mind with the world?

Don't get me wrong. Of course most writers want to make some money from what they write, and if you're reading this book, then you're probably one of them. I am, too. But if making money is your sole goal, you might want to re-think your choice of career. Try engineering.

Are you writing because someone said you should? Do you have a message to spread to the world? What is important to you? And if you don't really have a good idea yet on why you want to write and publish your work, keep thinking on it. If you're a writer, you'll find a reason to write. Dig deep.

Think about your priorities in life. Maybe it's important to you to provide for your family or maybe you've always dreamed of being famous. A lot of authors need a creative outlet so they don't go crazy in their day-to-day life. Not going insane can be a pretty strong motivating force.

Setting Timelines

You have some goals in mind, but when do you plan to accomplish them? Giving yourself realistic deadlines will help you narrow your focus even more. Think about the big goals we've been brainstorming and decide when you think you can actually get there. Is it in twenty-five years? Ten? By your next high school reunion?

Are there any goals that you absolutely have to have a deadline for? What are those deadlines? Are they firm? Can you build some leeway into them?

The Ten-Year Plan

You've thought about your goals, why you have them, and when you'd like to accomplish them. All of these deep thoughts have been building to the very basics of a business plan. I call it the ten-year plan. Even though you'll actually be thinking about the next twenty-five years, Twenty-five-year plan doesn't have the same ring to it and it sounds much more daunting.

Let's start with a one-year plan. In your writing career what would you like to accomplish in the next twelve months?

Here are some goal setting categories to think about.

- Writing
- Career
- Honing My Craft
- Time Management
- Financial
- Me Time

Start with a writing goal. Would you like to finish a manuscript? Finish two? Write a novella? Write an article for a magazine? Write

100,000 words? Write fifty-two blog posts? Be specific and realistic. What do you hope to accomplish and what can you actually complete in the next three hundred and sixty-five days?

Next, think about a career goal for this year. What can you do to help further your career as a writer besides write? Join a national, local, or online writing group? Establish a street team? Get a website up and running? Buy a laptop? Read a business book? Open a business banking account? Clean your office?

I like to include goals to hone my craft in my plans. They can be part of your career goals, but I separate them because they're important to me. Part of being a good writer is continually find ways to be a better writer. You might want to include how many or what kind of writing books you'll read this year. Or how many workshops you'd like to attend (online or in person). Maybe you'd like to join a critique group or go to a writing retreat or conference. Even if you're a multi-published, internationally acclaimed author, you can always improve your craft. A great way to do that is to teach what you know. Think about holding a workshop for other writers. You'd be surprised how much you'll get out of it.

Time management goals can help you keep track of how much time you spend on all the aspects of your business. You can include your time-management goals within the individual categories, or have separate goals. You may start with time to write. How many days a week and hours a day can you dedicate to writing? Now that you know there is more to the business of writing besides getting words on the page, think about the other activities you have to spend your time on. How much time will you spend on social media? Marketing? Research? Reading?

Financial goals are important, too. Are you planning to make money from writing this year? Well, how much? If you're not going to make money from your words on the page do you have any other alternative income streams that are related to the writing business? If you plan on a business loss this year, how much are your losses and what are you spending the money on? (Books are my biggest business expense every year. Workshops and conferences come in at a close second.) Think about what you'd like to be able to buy with the money you're going to make. That can be a financial goal too. Would you like to make enough money to buy a car, or Taco Bell for lunch? You decide.

Finally, you might think about what I call the Me Time goals. Don't forget to take care of yourself in all this business. You are your top asset, after all. There is no business without you. So take care of you. Goals for this might include asking the family to fend for themselves for dinner one night a week, so you can read and write. Maybe you want a weekend away at a hotel to hide away and write, write, write. How about a yoga and meditation class to help clear your mind and fend off writer's block? You know what you need. Plan for it.

Is there anything else in your writing business or writing life that is important to you? It could be anything from making new friends to finding a job in the publishing industry. Add that to your goals list too.

Three-, Five-, Ten- and Twenty-Five-Year Plans

You've thought a lot about very specific goals for this year. Now you should do the same thing for what you'd like to accomplish in three years. Think of all those same categories and see what you think you can do by the year 20_ _. When you have those done, think about a five-year plan.

Done with that? How about a ten-year plan? Great work, but keep going. Remember those really big goals we worked on at the beginning of this chapter? Work those into your twenty-five year plan.

The final part of your ten-year plan is a review. Make sure all of your goals flow together, to get you where you ultimately want to be. Then each year, when you put your new strategies together, review those goals and evaluate. Check to see what you accomplished and what you didn't. Work out why you made your goals and why didn't for the good, the bad, and the ugly.

Then re-evaluate for the upcoming year, three years, five years, ten years, and twenty-five years. Do you still have the same goals? Some will probably be the same. But the publishing industry, she is a-changing, so your goals probably will too. Each year you work a ton being a writer, you'll learn more and more about the industry. This will likely have an effect on your goals. Make sure to evaluate and update where you aim to be and how you will get there. Check in occasionally on how you're doing on your journey to becoming that writer.

When you've got your goals written down, print them out and hang them up where you will see them every day. If you have an office where you write, hang them there. If you write at a coffee shop every day, print them out smaller and tape them to the back of your laptop. You can even tape them to your bathroom mirror, so it's the first thing you see every morning, and the last thing you see before going to bed. Wherever you put them, take the time to look at those goals every day and use them to think about what you are doing. Is what you are doing helping you to accomplish those goals? If not, rethink what you're doing and focus on making your writing career everything you want it to be.

A couple of examples of goal-based plans follow in the next section. The ideas there may or may not be anything like yours, they are simply to illustrate what an intense yearly goal plan might look like.

Example Goals Plan

Here is an example of a detailed goal plan for a pre-published author who is writing novels.

One-year plan: By the end of this year, I will...

Writing:

Complete two full-length manuscripts (100,000 words each) and one novella (30,000 words).

Have those manuscripts critiqued/beta read.

Develop three new ideas for stories.

Complete NaNoWriMo.

Join people on Twitter for #1k1hr.

Career:

Send twenty query letters to agents for each manuscript.

Get rejections.

Start a blog and update it once a week.

Attend every monthly meeting of my local writing group.

Honing My Craft:

Take four online workshops (one per quarter).

Read four craft books (one per quarter).

Attend the national writing conference with writers' workshops.

Teach one workshop.

Time Management:

Write every weekday evening from 6–8 p.m.

Write Saturday and Sunday mornings, at least twice a month.

Be on social media about an hour a day (not much more, not much less).

Financial:

File taxes claiming writing as a business.

Make $100 from teaching or presenting workshops.

Get a separate credit card for business expenses only.

Me Time:

Attend writers' group annual retreat in the mountains.

Read for an hour every night before bed.

Have lunch/dinner with writer friends once a month.

Three-year plan: Three years from now, I will be...

Writing:

Completing two full-length manuscripts (100,000 words each) and one novella (30,000 words) each year
Having those manuscripts critiqued/beta read.
Developing three new ideas for stories.

Career:
Working with an agent to sell my debut novel.
Guest blogging to help establish my brand, beyond my own website.
Guest lecturing for my local writing group.
Self-publish a novella or non-fiction book.
Register a DBA with my state.

Honing My Craft:

Taking two online workshops for debut authors.
Reading two publishing books.
Attending national writing conference with writers' workshops AND attending one readers' conference.
Teaching a workshop at my national writing conference.

Time Management:

Writing every weekday morning from 6—7 a.m. and weekday evening from 6–8 p.m.
Writing Saturday and Sunday mornings at least twice a month.
On social media about an hour a day (not much more, not much less).

Spend an hour a weekday working on marketing and strategies for my debut release.

Financial:

File taxes claiming writing as a business.
Make $250 from teaching or presenting workshops.
Make $100/month in self-publishing.

Me Time:

Attend writers' group annual retreat in the mountains.
Read for an hour every night before bed.
Have lunch/dinner with writer friends once a month.

Five-year plan: Five years from now, I will be...

Writing:

Completing three full length manuscripts (100,000 words each) and two novellas (30,000 words) each year.

Having those manuscripts beta read.

Developing five new ideas for stories.

Career:

Have sold debut novel to traditional publisher.

Working with an agent on multi-book contracts and foreign rights.

Guest blogging with other authors and spending time on review sites to establish discoverability and market.

Present a workshop at national conference.

Enter national writing competition.

Self-publish a novel and a novella.

Establish an LLC.

Have a newsletter.

Create a street team.

Honing My Craft:

Taking two online workshops in a new (to me) style of writing or genre.

Reading two publishing books.

Attending and presenting at national writing conference.

Establish online group of published writers within my genre to discuss writing and the business.

Time Management:

Writing every weekday from 9–5.

Writing Saturday and Sunday mornings at least twice a month.

On social media about an hour a day (not much more, not much less).

Spend an hour a weekday working on marketing and strategies for next release.

Financial:

File taxes as an LLC.

Make $1,000/month in self-publishing.

Earn out advance on debut novel.

Me Time:

Attend writers' group annual retreat in the mountains.

Read for an hour every night before bed.

Have lunch/dinner with writer friends once a month.

Ten-year plan: Ten years from now, I will be...

Writing:

Completing four full-length manuscripts (100,000 words each) and three novellas (30,000 words) each year.

Having those manuscripts beta read.

Developing five new ideas for stories.

Career:

Have two established series with traditional publishers, each with two releases a year (including novellas).

Working with an agent on multi-book contracts, foreign rights, and movie rights.

Self-publishing backlist of books with rights re-acquired.

Present a workshop at national conference.

Win national writing competition.

Self-publish a novel and a novella.

Be a featured author at a readers' convention.

Have a master's degree.

Have an assistant.

Have a publicist.

Honing My Craft:

Write a craft book for authors.

Reading two publishing books.

Attending and presenting at national writing conference.

Time Management:

Writing every weekday from 9–5.

Spend an hour a day meeting with my team (assistant, publicist, etc.).

Financial:

Have an accountant.

Make $5,000/month in self-publishing.

Make $250,000 in advances and royalties.

Buy a home.

Me Time:

Read for an hour before bed every night.

Have lunch/dinner with writer friends once a month.

Twenty-Five year plan: Twenty-five years from now, I will be...

Writing:

Completing three full-length manuscripts (100,000 words each) and three novellas (30,000 words) each year.

Having those manuscripts beta read.

Developing five new ideas for stories.

Career:

Have 100 novels printed by a traditional publisher.

Be translated in fifteen languages and have movies made from five books.

Present a workshop at national conference.

Win national writing competition.

Have 25 self-published novels and 50 self-published novellas.

Be a corporation.

Have my own fan convention.

Honing My Craft:

Be an editor at a publishing house.

Have five writing books in print.

Time Management:

Have an accountant.

Make $10,000/month in self-publishing.

Make $2.5 million in advances and royalties.

Have two vacation homes.

Me Time:

Read for an hour before bed every night.

Have lunch/dinner with writer friends once a month.

Have two or more vacations abroad a year.

Goals Template

Now it's your turn to take a shot at writing your goals. You can download this template at

www.CoffeeBreakSocialMedia.com/Books/Resources.

CHAPTER 6

What to Include in Your Business Plan

Beauty and the Beast

I'm a very right-brained person, with a left-brained analyst hiding inside of my hypothalamus. I love to craft, read romance, and wear pretty clothes. But hiding just behind the pom-poms and eyeshadow is a data analyst. I could spend hours playing with spreadsheets and dissecting texts. But, shhhh. Don't tell.

There's a little bit of work for both sides of the brain in creating the sections that follow. You can put all your information into a spreadsheet, or type it in a Word document that you later print out and keep in a binder. Go right ahead. But if that gives you the heebie-jeebies, think about creating a visual business plan. I highly recommend The Right-Brain Business Plan by Jennifer Lee for more ideas on how to make an artistic plan.

If this idea appeals to you, collect some images from magazines or the Internet, photos, drawings, doodles, or anything else that speaks to your goals.

Here are a few ideas for putting them into a workable plan.

- Create vision boards. Start with a bulletin board, or even a piece of cardboard. As you work through this section of your plan, paste images or words onto the board that have meaning for you.

- Make a picture book plan. Take an old, but larger, children's board book. Make sure there are enough pages for the sections of your plan. Paste paper over the pages and put images and words on each page that represent the goals and ideas for your plan.

- Put your plan in a box. Get a smallish cardboard box and paste images and words on the box, and then fill the box with cards for each section of your plan.

- Wear your plan. Get a large light-colored scarf and use permanent markers or puffy paint and draw pictures and words that correspond to the parts of your plan. Or, if you're into jewelry making, create beads or charms with words and pictures for your goals and plans. Every time you wear these, it will help you focus on your plan. It's also a great conversation starter.

For all of your visual business plans, I suggest that you keep some sort of pocket or folder in which you keep some written details of the plan — maybe colorful note cards, sticky notes, or pages from a legal pad folded into origami cranes. You decide.

A Formal Business Plan

A traditional formal business plan typically has three main parts with seven sub-sections. They have very official and business-y sounding names like Executive Summary and Competitive Analysis. I'm falling asleep already.

Being an author entrepreneur isn't the traditional start-up business, so you won't be writing the same old boring sleeping pill. You wouldn't write the same book as someone else, so don't write the same business plan.

To help make the whole process a little more fun, I've given the sections bookish terms. They are named for components of books and bookstores, so whether you write fiction or non, they'll work for you.

Once you understand what kind of information you'll put in the different sections, you can name them whatever you want. Don't let the vocabulary intimidate you. Remember, I'll walk you through each step of writing the plan. In each of the steps I've provided considerations for the different phases of your author's journey and the various paths to publishing. You can also do the sections of the plan in any order you want. If you're excited about creating an action plan, do the **Chapters** section first. If you're dying to get a marketing plan together, work on **Get in the Bag**. You'll probably want to save **The Bank** for last, since it will be easier once you know what you'll be spending and making money on.

If there is a section that makes you nauseated just thinking about it, save it. Don't let the time and research you'll need to do overwhelm you or make you sick. Just do a little bit at a time. Just like when you write a book.

There are three main parts of your business plan. Hmm, similar to the three-act structure. Interesting how art follows life (or vice versa).

Remember some of the sections you should be able to do in a coffee break. A few sections you'll need to take a few coffee breaks or even a lunch break to get your ideas in order.

Act I — The Book

The business concept is your first act. In Act I, you'll talk about what kind of writing you plan to do and how you'll be successful. You'll organize that information into a few sections.

The Blurb (traditionally called The Executive Summary)

The back of a book gives you a general idea of what the story or ideas inside are about. Same goes for your business plan. This summary gives the main points of your plan — the big picture. The ten-question Coffee Break Business plan will be similar to your blurb. You can do it first, or last. If you do it first, it might give you focus for the rest of the plan, but you can write the rest of the plan first and do the blurb last when you've solidified all of your ideas and have them in print.

The Cover (traditionally known as the business description or company overview)

Take a look at a good book cover. You should get a sense of quite a few things about it, like the genre, its intended audience, and in a print book, about how many pages are in it. This section of your plan will give some details about the writing business and where your place in that world is.

The Acknowledgements Page (an operations and management plan)

It takes a village, or so the saying goes. The same is true to create a book for publication. In this section, you'll detail your writing process and who is involved, like critique partners, beta readers, etc. If you'd like to work with an agent, editor, publisher, proofreader, cover artist, printer, or the other plethora of people who go into getting your book on the shelf, put them here too. You can also include advisors, mentors or people in professional organizations you belong to.

The Chapters (a design and development plan, the action plan)

This section is the meat of the project, just like the chapters in a book. You'll take all those pretty goals you made in step two and apply the SMART philosophy to them. SMART stands for specific, measurable, attainable, realistic, and timely. Then you can make yourself some to-do lists to get those goals accomplished.

Act II — The Bookstore

The bookstore section is where you'll consider who your potential readers are and who your competition is in your genre(s). You'll also look at how you can position yourself and your books to beat out the competition. This is the part of the plan where you discuss how to build your platform. The sections to do this in are:

The Shelves (the industry)

It is a good idea to be aware of what's going on in the publishing industry and in your genre. In this section, you'll give an overall view of trends and the future of books and book buying.

Your Shelf (competitive analysis)

You don't just need to know about publishing in general, but what's going on in your genre. Here you'll evaluate who your ideal reader is, who else is writing and selling books like yours, and determine how you can stand out among the millions of other books people buy every day.

Getting in the Bag (marketing strategies)

We all wish our publishers would spend a million dollars in co-op money to get our book placed at the front of all the stores, or we'd get a TV ad on during the Superbowl, or maybe an appearance on Oprah's book club.

But in reality we have to do a majority of our marketing ourselves. So you might as well have a plan, right? This section will also include information on building your brand, your social media, and promotions.

Act III — The Bank

The bank section discusses, well, money. How much money can you make being a writer? It all depends on how much you have to spend. Budgets and spreadsheets and taxes, oh my! This part doesn't have to be scary. You don't have to use complicated software that produces P&L statements. But you can plan for income and get an idea of how much you'll be spending to get your book on the shelves. I will provide some templates if you do want to use a spreadsheet. This way you don't have to start from scratch.

CHAPTER 7

Time to Write Your Plan

Now that you have an overview of the sections of the business plan, it's time to dig and and put your own ideas on paper (or computer.)

The next five sections in this chapter detail exactly what to do, step-by-step. There are lots of questions for you to consider, and a few things to research. Remember, the point is to take coffee breaks, maybe before or after your regular writing time, to get this work done.

A few items in the list will take you more than fifteen minutes. Break those up into a few breaks or if you get really into it, take a few hours on your day off to give it your all.

Have your ten-question Coffee Break Business Plan from chapter four and the goals you wrote in chapter five on hand. You'll want to refer back to and let them guide your strategies for the rest of the plan.

You'll need a notebook, whiteboard, notecards and corkboard, or giant piece of construction paper and something to write with. Make it pretty if you want.

There's a functional template at

www.coffeebreaksocialmedia.com/books/resources you can download with all the sections all ready to go if you want something ready made for this task.

Okay. Ready, Set, Go!

The Blurb

The blurb gives you the big picture. A glimpse at the whole story, but not the details. If you do your blurb at the beginning of your plan, you can refer back to it while constructing the rest of the sections. If you decide to do it at the end, you can use all the other parts of the plan to summarize. Either way works.

This is where you describe your dream career as an author. Talk about what kind of author you aspire to be. These are your ideals, but they are realistic ones.

You'll see some of these same questions in the rest of the sections. Remember, this is a summary of the rest of your plan. These answers should be short and to the point. When you're finished you can put your answers into one or two paragraphs.

Answer these questions:

What genre(s) do you write?

It's okay if you write in more than one genre, or even more than one sub-genre (or even think you might want to someday). It's also a great idea if you're starting out to focus on one genre until you feel you've mastered it. Then move on to more projects. If you choose to write in multiple genres, think about whether you'll need multiple pen names (which likely also means multiple social media accounts). This is a hugely debated question and you'll need to do some research and soul-searching to decide the answer for yourself.

How will you publish?

Your plan will be very different whether you publish traditionally, do it yourself, or if you do a hybrid of the two.

How many books will you publish a year?

How much money will you make from publishing?

Check out The Bank section for more information on figuring out your income.

What kind of accolades will you earn for your work (publishing awards, *USA Today* and *New York Times* bestseller's lists, a pat on the back from your mom, etc.)?

Who are you writing for?

This could mean yourself, family, and friends. But then think about who your target market is. I'll cover more about your ideal reader in the marketing section, so just answer generally here. A few examples might be, middle-aged soccer moms, financial planning enthusiasts, or wine snobs.

The Muse

From the summary, you can develop your author mission statement. Your mission statement can be very inspirational, which is why I called it the Muse. This is one or two sentences that sum up you and your goals for a successful writing career. Think of this as your mantra, or the logline for your writing career. Your books have loglines, why shouldn't you?

Whenever you're stuck, feeling down about writing or getting published, or need a jumpstart to your day, get this sentence back out and see if it doesn't get your imagination running again.

Try to give your muse value. That can mean financial value, but can also be personal values — like family or life philosophies. If being able to support your family financially is an important value to you, include that. If you need to write just to stay sane, include that. If it's important that your friends and family are proud of you, say that. These are your core beliefs as they relate to your writing career. Include them in your muse statement so that it is valuable to you.

The name of the muse game is inspiration. If you think it, you believe it. If you believe it, you are it. If you use the present simple tense, i.e. I am instead of I want, I will be, or I can, then you're one step closer to believing you are the writer of your dreams. Another part of inspiration is to use those big dream goals. If you want to be a best-selling author, include that in your muse statement. Whatever your true aspirations are, use them here.

Woo-hoo! You're getting excited now, right? Okay, not to be a downer, but the inspiration you put in this all-important sentence must also be realistic. You might be tempted to say you'll be making a million dollars with your writing next week, but unless you're already a multi-published author whose last royalty statement came in at $999,999, this isn't very realistic. A million dollars can absolutely be your goal, but be honest with yourself about when that might actually happen. If it happens sooner than that, then yay!

You also need to be specific with the goals in your statement. Don't say you mean to write a bunch of books that people really like. Do say you write four books a year, or fifty books, or one book that gets five-star reviews and wins your genre's industry award.

Here's an example:

I am a financially successful author who shares award-winning stories of love and adventure with readers around the world.

Let's evaluate this muse statement's components.

Does it have value? It does say financially successful and award-winning, both of which hold some value.

Is it inspirational? The sentence is in the present tense, and assuming the author isn't already financially successful and winning awards, it does have modest goals. The part about readers around the world also speaks to the idea that the author wants to be read by more than just family and friends.

Are the goals plausible? Sure they are.

The biggest problem with this muse statement is that it isn't very specific. It has the other three components, but they seem ho-hum because there is no specificity.

Try rewriting this statement with some specific goals for these words: financially successful, shares, award-winning, and around the world.

Do you have a clearer vision of where this author wants to be?

Now try your hand at writing your own.

Your muse statement can go through lots of drafts and incarnations. If you add a new dimension to your business plan, you might need to update your statement.

You can have more than one mission statement, too. If you find creating a mission statement motivational, consider creating them for different parts of your life and career. You can have one for your writing career, your marketing efforts, your financial goals, your family life, spiritual life, your health, or anything else that is important to you.

The Cover

In The Cover section, you'll be describing your business. Here's where you talk about the purpose of your business, what kind of products you'll produce, and how. Of course your business is writing, but what kind of writing? You'll have to do a little bit of research to answer some of the questions for this section, but for your first draft, it's perfectly okay for you to guess. Once you're ready for some content editing, you can go back and find the answers you weren't sure about. You'll recognize a few questions here from previous section, The Blurb. But in The Cover, I'll be asking you to go into the answers more in depth.

Do you write fiction? If so, what genre(s)? What length?

The average full-length fiction novel is approximately 100,000 words (which translates to around 350 pages). What length is normal for the genre in which you write? Harlequin category romance can be as little as 50,000 words, whereas some of the epic fantasy novels come in at 300,000. Short stories or novellas can be anywhere from 2,500 to 40,000 words. Know the average word count for your genres and aim for them. It will make your books more marketable.

Do you write non-fiction? If so, on what topic(s)? What length?

Non-fiction titles have the advantage of being any length you want. Overall, they tend to be shorter than novels, but some biographies and histories can rival epic fantasies. Look at other titles similar to yours and check out their page counts to see what will be marketable in your genre.

Who is your proposed publisher?

If it's a traditional publisher you're after, select a few. Be specific if you're planning on publishing with a particular imprint. For example, you might be targeting Hachette, but if you write romance, you'll want to submit to their Grand Central Forever imprint. Definitely take a look at the imprints of the Big Six/Big Five for your genre. If you don't know who these mythical Big Six are (they aren't an athletic conference) there is a post on the Coffee Break Social Media blog. If you've ever bought a traditionally published book it's likely you've purchased something from the Big Six. They are a group of six (now five, since Random House and Penguin have merged) New York based publishers. They all have imprints, which means a group that only publishes certain genres.

Also, take a look at smaller publishing houses and digital-first or digital-only publishers. The best way to find the publisher(s) to target is by taking a look at the books you like and see who publishes them.

Self-publishers must decide if they want to simply publish under their own names or if they want to register a trade name, start an LLC, or form a corporation for their publishing company. You should also detail what parts of the publishing process you will direct yourself and what parts you will outsource. The writing will be yours, but you can outsource the cover design, formatting, editing, marketing, uploads to various sales sites, filing the copyright, obtaining an ISBN, and more.

If you are self-publishing, what software or platform will you use to produce your books?

There are more ways to publish on your own than you can imagine. You can write in any word processing program. There are free ones, like the open source office suites. Apache's Open Office, Libre Office, and

KOffice are all free. KOffice and NeoOffice are both available for Mac, although NeoOffice costs a modest ten dollars a year.

Once you finish writing, there are programs like Calibre that convert your books to the various formats from a Word document, and there are programs like Scrivener that you can use to both write and format your book. If you'd like to sell print books, there are businesses like Lulu where you can have copies made, or you can use something like CreateSpace from Amazon to print books on demand.

If you self-publish, where will you sell your books?

Amazon is the monster we love to hate, but if you want to sell books to more than just your grandma, you're gonna have to be on Amazon. Think about whether you'll use Amazon's KDP Select program, too. There's more about this in the *Get in the Bag* (marketing strategies) section.

Other very popular places to sell your book online are Barnes & Noble, Kobo, and Apple's iBook store. (Although you'll need a Mac, or a friend with a Mac, to format and upload your book for the iStore.)

Smashwords will not only sell your book on their site, but can format and distribute your book to all the other major e-tailers too. There has also been a surge of create-your-own online bookstore sites lately, so you can sell directly to the reader. Check out Gumroad for an easy, free-to-set-up and no-fuss online bookstore of your own.

If you decide to sell print books, you'll likely have to do most of the legwork yourself. There are distribution options for self-pubbers. CreateSpace has an option for expanded distribution channels that will cost you just a few dollars to sign up. You can sell your print books at local bookstores. Independent stores are more likely than larger chains to carry your books if you ask. However, if you do an in-store signing or book talk, they might even carry copies of your book.

Don't forget about other venues for book sales. Depending on your topic, you might be able to sell your books in specific local businesses. If you've got speaking engagements, like workshops or lectures, you should definitely have your books for sale there. But don't forget about charging sales tax.

Will you be publishing in print or digitally, or both?

Being traditionally published doesn't always mean getting your book in print. A lot of the Big Six have digital-first or digital-only imprints. There are quite a few small presses that also only sell digital books. Traditional publishing also doesn't necessarily mean digital books either. For the most part publishers have gotten on the e-book bandwagon, but there are a few of the old guard that wish paperbacks had never been invented, much less the digital revolution. Be sure you know what formats you'll get with the publishers you're targeting.

Many self-published books are only available digitally. If you want your book in print, you'll need to get it printed. The best option these days is print-on-demand (POD). Only when a customer orders your book is a copy printed. POD books are generally a little pricier because the printer can't save a jillion dollars printing thousands of your books at one go. Those mass-market paperbacks we all love to read for $3.49–7.99 a pop were printed, well, in mass. Print runs for traditional mass-market paperbacks are anywhere from 10,000 to 250,000 books. CreateSpace is Amazon's easy-to-use POD supplier.

Stay away from vanity publishers, which are companies that charge you to print books unless your book really is just for you and grandma.

They are expensive, and serious authors and readers find them lacking legitimacy. Although, to be fair, Herman Melville used a vanity press for Moby-Dick. Granted, he was seen as a failure as an author in his own lifetime. But now? You'd be hard pressed to find very many people in the world who haven't heard of the great white whale.

What qualifies you to write these books or in this genre?

Things like degrees, relevant work history, real world experience, awards, and recognitions are all good to have in this section.

Listing your qualifications gives you and anyone who might review your plan a good look at the experience in your background that will help make you successful. It gives you and your plan more credibility.

If you don't have a degree in English, haven't worked in the publishing industry, and don't have any awards or recognitions that are relevant to your writing career, answer this question: What made you want to become a writer, or what pushed you to write this particular book?

Maybe you've read extensively in your genre. That counts. If you've been reading Sci-Fi for the last twenty years, you've gained a certain expertise in that genre. If you read business book after business book to help you run your company, advance in the corporate world, or just for the fun and knowledge, that counts too.

Have you been telling stories since you were old enough to speak? Pull out that report card from your second grade teacher that says you're a "lovely child but need to spend less time in your imaginary world and more time focusing on multiplication tables."

How about those twelve short stories/full-length novels/half-finished manuscripts shoved in your desk drawer? We call that years and years' worth of practice.

Don't forget real world experience. If you're writing a novel about an MIA soldier making his way home from Vietnam, and you were in the military yourself, that's real world experience that makes you an expert. If you owned a sandwich franchise and are writing a murder mystery that takes place in a restaurant, that too is experience that qualifies you to write this book.

This is a good place to look at obstacles and contingency plans. If these plans don't work out, what can you do to overcome those obstacles? You may want to have a completely separate section for these ideas, or you might just put in a sentence or two for each area about possible obstacles and what your plans are to overcome those.

Acknowledgements Page

Who does what in your business? Most authors spend hours and hours all by themselves writing in their caves. But sometimes you have to pop your head out and ask other people to have some input on your writing or getting it published. Anyone who has helped you with your business, from writing to web design, goes here. It can also be a handy place to keep their contact information. This is the place to detail who those people are and what they've done for you. Plus, it will make your acknowledgements page or your industry award speech easier to write.

Who owns your business?

If you have created a legal entity, like a Limited Liability Company (LLC) or registered a trade name (DBA), you would also list that information here. Go big here and list where your business is located, who owns your business, and what assets your business owns.

There are plenty of authors who have writing partners, or co-authors. Whether or not you have a formal partnership agreement, you should list here the people you rely onto get words on the page before you publish.

Who helps you with your work-in-progress?

Lots of authors have critique partners or groups. Maybe you use beta readers or brainstormers.

Do you have any advisors?

Do you belong to a writers' group that helps you with professional development, or maybe they just keep you sane in this crazy publishing world? Do you have a mentor who helps you understand all the steps in the process to getting your books on the shelves? Even if you just get together for coffee or lunch and talk shop with some other writers, you can put them in this part of your plan.

Do you outsource any of your publishing process?

Both traditional and self-published authors might use a developmental editor, a line editor, a copy editor, and a proofreader before they submit their books for query or publishing.

If you're self-published you might also have someone for cover design, formatting, uploading, and more. Whether these are individuals or businesses, keep their information here.

What other professional services are you using?

Do you have a business bank account? How about a webmaster? Someone who does graphic arts for your online presence? Social media consultants? Accountant? Lawyer? Agent? Publicist? Assistant?

The Chapters

The Chapters are the longest and most important part of your book and it will be for your business plan too. This is the section where you write what you're going to actually do to make your goals happen.

Book Production Schedule

Time to get really honest with yourself. How many words can you actually write in a day, week, month, or year? Is it enough to accomplish your goals? If not, you have a couple of choices. Re-evaluate your goals, or find a way to up your word count. If you're a new writer, or an old writer who isn't yet published, now is the time to hold yourself to deadlines. If you've never written a lot of words in a short amount of time, try joining NaNoWriMo (aka NAtional NOvel WRIting MOnth). 50,000 words, 30 days, and 400,000 of your closest insane crazy writer friends (www.NaNoWriMo.org).

It's a great idea to keep track of how many words or pages you write every day. Spreadsheets work great for this, and there are a couple of templates you can download at www.coffeebreaksocialmedia.com/Books/Resources. You can also add widgets to your website. There are also all kinds of websites that you can track your progress on. I like pretty charts and graphs (they make me feel like I've accomplished something), so one of my favorite sites is StoryToolz.com.

If you got the whole wordage thing down, think about creating a schedule for yourself.

Here are a few items to think about for your book production schedule. Only you know your process (although it could change) and what deadlines you can make. Any of these dates could be broken up into multiple dates if you work chapter by chapter or by section. You decide what works for you.

- Plotting completed by date.
- First draft completed by date.
- To critique partners by date.
- To beta readers by date.
- Revised draft completed date.
- To agent by date.
- To editor by date. (This could include your publishing house editor if you're traditionally published, or it could mean a freelance developmental editor, copy/line editor, or a proofreader.) You might have more than one date here, depending on your path to publication or your publisher.
- Final draft completed date:

You might want to get a big desk or wall calendar to put up right in front of your computer. If your deadlines are up there (and big) in front of you every day, you can't say you didn't remember. Hold yourself accountable. You can also input the dates into an online calendar. Outlook, Yahoo, Google, and others have calendar options available (that come with reminders you can set).

Don't let your schedule add super stress to your life, though. If you can't make a deadline, be honest about it with yourself and with anyone you owe your manuscript to. Will there be repercussions for pushing your deadlines? Yep. These are anything from never finishing your book, to getting your release date pushed back a year before your publisher can fit you back into the schedule.

Here are some additional deadlines to put on your book production schedule after you've finished the writing:

- Query letters sent to agents and editors — follow up with agents and editors
- Information to cover artist — approval of cover art
- Manuscript to formatter
- Marketing campaign: There's a whole other section for your marketing plan, so don't detail all of those dates here. You can just put in some major milestones.
- Formatted manuscript with cover to various e-tailers (i.e. Amazon, Smashwords, etc.)

The Author-Entrepreneur Checklist

The following is a list of suggestions, besides writing, you might want to do or have to be a professional author. You don't need them all at once, so you might add some of these to your pretty book production schedule for when you plan to start, and finish the items on this list that appeal to you. If you'd like to download the checklist without the explanations, it is available at

www.coffeebreaksocialmedia.com/Books/Resources.

Assets

Do you have what you need to actually write every day, like say, a computer? It's okay if you don't when you first start out. Write on legal pads, or hit the library and save your work on a flash drive or in a cloud system. But eventually you're probably going to need a dedicated computer for writing.

You decide what else you might need beyond that. A printer? A desk?

Your online platform

A website.

You've got to have a website. Sorry. But it doesn't have to cost you thousands of dollars. If you're just starting out in your writing career, think about getting yourself a WordPress blog to start. It can act like a webpage until you have the means and motives to get something more. *The Coffee Break Guide to Author Websites* by Diane Whiddon can help you work your way through the minefield of creating your own website.

A dedicated professional author email address.

Something that has your pen name, and if you can, matches your website URL. If you can get an email address along with your domain, that's perfect. Example: PenName@PenName.com. If you can't, that's okay too, just make sure your email address is simple, easy to remember, and based on your pen name.

A blog.

You don't have to have one, but you might like a place to announce your new releases and do cover reveals and offer fun stuff for your readers.

It is a great place to build your platform, but if you know you can't dedicate yourself to blogging on a regular basis, don't bother.

Other social media sites (Facebook, Twitter, Goodreads, Amazon, Pinterest and more).

Social media is a fact of life for the majority of authors today. It's the greatest free marketing tool available and it gives your fans and readers a chance to interact with their favorite author. If the whole social media thing scares you, check out my book *The Coffee Break Guide to Social Media for Writers.* It's all about how to be successful on social media and still have time to write.

Professional

Business cards are perfect for when you have an in-person contact and want to give that person a takeaway. Whenever I say I'm a writer, people always ask what I write. If it's something they are interested in, I will definitely give them a business card so they can remember to look me up later. You may also attend conferences (which are great for networking, professional development workshops, and good fun!) and you'll want to take a ton of business cards to those.

A business bank account is a good idea to help separate your author expenses from the rest of your life. Your accountant will like you better, and so will the IRS. You don't really need a business bank account until you start getting those first royalty checks. Most local banks are more than happy to let you open a second checking account and it doesn't have to be a business checking account (which usually has extra fees associated with them).

If you're not ready for a whole extra bank account, you might consider getting a credit card specifically for your business expenses. Don't let credit worry you. All the big credit card companies offer a pre-paid credit card that you can use for your business if you don't want to open a new account.

A PO box will come in really handy when you get raving fans trying to stalk you and/or helping you keep some privacy in your new public life.

A publicity photo is important to have for your website, your social media accounts, and that cool author photo on the back flap of your latest release. They don't have to be expensive, but they should at least look professional... even if they aren't. No, you can't cut out your ex from that great picture of you from high school. Get something current. Nothing is worse than those glamour shots from the 80s, or a blurry church photo from ten years ago on an author website.

Professional Development

A very important part of a writer's journey is honing your craft, staying up to date on trends in the publishing industry, and staying sane. Successful authors continually hone their craft. Successful business people continually hone their business strategies. How do we do that? Professional development.

Writing isn't like most other industries. There's not a whole lot of secrets and espionage. Writers like to share when they learn something cool, or when they become experts in a particular skill. Thus there are lots of books, workshops, conferences, and professional associations for writers. So what are you going to do to educate yourself? What skills would you like to develop? What books are available to help you? What writers' organizations offer workshops for your genre or for a skill you'd like to develop? Are there any local writers' groups that offer workshops or meetings?

If you don't have a particular skill you know you'd like to work on, you might give yourself a schedule and study whatever takes your fancy at the moment. Or, if you have a lot of skills to work on, make a list of them and some resources to help you work your way through the items.

No idea at all what to work on? Hit the library and check out their section on writing books. Pick something that sounds interesting to you.

Shelves

So, you walk into a bookstore (or peruse the virtual bookshelves of Amazon, etc.), pick up a couple of interesting titles from the shelves, and buy them. But why did you choose those books and not any of the other ones on the shelves?

There's a lot of competition. So why would anyone choose your book?

Time to figure out just that very thing.

You'll have to do a little research for this section, but you can use Google for a lot of it, and you'll get to go to the bookstore (which is my favorite kind of homework). Plus, I think you'll be surprised how much you already know.

This is the part that always scared me. How in the world am I supposed to find out information about the competition? Don't get paralyzed with fear here. You don't have to call up other authors and ask them about their incomes, or ask giant publishing houses to tell you how many books they print every year. You don't even need to know what the annual sales volume is for your genre. What you're looking for here are trends, news, strengths, weaknesses, and similarities.

The bookstore represents the writing and publishing industry as a whole. The individual shelves are your genre(s) and your shelf is for your book.

The Bookstore Shelves

Let's start with a look at the publishing industry as a whole.

What's the big buzz over the last few years in publishing? There's been a lot. But what news relates to you and your writing career? Maybe it's something about how anyone can be an author now, through the path of self-publishing. Or maybe you're interested in the decline of brick-and-mortar bookstores and the rise of online retailers like Amazon. Are you interested in the fact that the Big Six publishers are more like the Big Five now and a lot of them have digital first imprints that don't require submittals by agents? (I am.)

Try searching for information about news and trends in publishing. Earmark the ones that really interest you. Think about the path you've chosen to get your work into the hands of readers and look for articles, blogs, and books that discuss self-publishing, traditional publishing, or a hybrid.

Look for information from a variety of sources. Look for updates from publishers themselves, other writers, readers, writing organization, news outlets, and even personal anecdotes. I've learned some of the most important lessons about the writing life from having coffee with a few other author friends.

Keep track of the articles and posts you read. You can make copies or print them out and keep a physical file, or create a bookmark folder for what you find online. Microsoft OneNote, EverNote, or Scrivener are great places for you to keep a virtual folder of all your research.

Don't let your research project keep you from doing your actual writing, however. Don't let it become the never-ending project. Give yourself a timeline or schedule of some sort for how many articles you'll read, and when. Maybe something like one a day or one a week, until you've read ten articles.

When you're ready, try to summarize what you've learned about the industry and include information about how that relates to your writing. You only need a few paragraphs for this section.

Just because you finish your business plan doesn't mean you should toss the research file. Keep reading, stay up to date, and keep sticking new articles in that file. Then when you review your plan each year, you can update it with any changes to the industry.

Your Shelf

Now that you have a good idea of what's happening in publishing and writing, it's time to narrow the focus to you. Your genre, your books. How do you fit in with the competition?

Another great source of current trends in publishing, and a direct line into your genre, is a trip to the bookstore or library. Peruse the shelves and see what they're offering.

Makes some notes on these questions as you look at the books:

- How big is the section of the bookstore for your genre?
- Is it one shelf or multiple aisles?
- If you have a couple hours to hang at the bookstore, how many customers enter your genre?
- How many actually walk away with a book? If you can, try this experiment on a few different days and at varying times to get a more accurate idea.
- Approximately how many books do they have in your genre?

- Are there other books like yours on those shelves?
- How many?
- What makes your book different from those or unique all together?
- Are there any books with the same title as yours?

Grab a few books from your genre from the shelves. If your genre is big, grab some from your sub-genre. Take them from several different places on the shelf, especially if your section is larger than a few shelves or has its very own section. Remember, book placement in stores is all about co-op money from the publishers, so don't just take the ones that are displayed prominently (although do grab a few of those), but make sure to take the ones from the bottom shelf in the back, too.

Choose at least ten books, if you can. You're going to examine these books to get a good picture of what a book looks like in your genre. You might want to take some notes. For this I have a downloadable worksheet at

www.coffeebreaksocialmedia.com/Books/Resources that you can use for your book study. If you are targeting a specific publisher for your books, try to get half of the books from that publisher. But be sure to check out other publishers, too.

- Take a look at the covers. What do you notice? Check out the kinds of pictures, fonts, text size, and colors they used. Are there quotes or reviews from other authors on the back covers? Have any of the books won awards that are noted on the front cover? Flip the book over. What's on the back cover? Is there a blurb about the book? Quotes from further reviews, similar authors, or testimonials? Are there any graphics? If the book is a hardcover with a jacket, open it up and check out what's on the inside front and back flaps.

- Open a book. What's on the first couple of pages? Blanks? Book blurbs, lists of other books by this author, book quotes, quotes from other authors, testimonials? Check out the copyright page. Note the publisher and the copyright. Look at books that are the most current in your genre. It will give you a good idea of what agents, editors, book buyers, and readers are purchasing. Note any other content that might be important at the beginning of the book before the actual chapters, like a foreword, table of contents, dedication, and more.

- How long is the book? How many pages?

- How is the book set up? In chapters, sections, or some other kind of format? Are there any blank pages? Are there headers, chapter titles, footers, footnotes? How long are the chapters or sections in the book?

- Are there any graphics in the book itself?

- Flip to the back of the book. What follows the book's main content? We call this the back matter. Is there a preview of another book? Is there a glossary of terms? Are there blurbs for other books by this author or other authors? Is there a letter from the author or a bio? Is there any other back matter?

Take a look at your notes and study it for trends, similarities to your book, unique qualities, and red flags (really unexpected content).

Now get online and go to your favorite e-tailer of books. If you don't have one, use Amazon, since they are the largest online book retailer.

Do the same thing you did at the bookstore, with the ten books. Search your genre, picking pick five books at random, and five books from the top-ten list for your category. Try not to use more than a couple of the same titles you looked at in the bookstore.

You may have to alter a few of the questions. Back cover and blurb will be on the book's Amazon page instead of on a non-existent back cover, and the jacket flaps just don't exist. Also, note for each book how many reviews it has (including the average score) and other books Amazon recommends for you. You can usually check out the first few pages in the book preview.

If you own any e-books, check out at least five of the most current ones for information on book set-up and back matter. If you don't own any, you might check to see if your local library does e-book lending. Most do. (Remember you don't have to own an e-book reader like a Kindle, Nook, or Kobo, to read e-books. You can read Kindle books right on your computer from the cloud at https://read.amazon.com/, or you can download the reader app of your choice to your computer. Have a smartphone or tablet? There's a reading app for all the major e-tailers for iPhone, Android and Blackberry. There's no excuse for not getting your hands on an e-book.)

Your Book

You now have a good idea of what's going on in publishing and writing in general, and some great specifics for your genre. So how do you fit into the big picture? Is your writing career on trend? Are you behind the times, or at the forefront of publishing? Is anyone publishing books like yours? If yes, who and how many (generally)? If not, does it look like there is a need for books like yours, or (be honest with yourself) is this going to be hard to sell?

Think about how you want to publish your books. Traditional or self-published? Print or digital? Is there a publisher for your work? If not, are you willing to self-publish? Or, if you are self-publishing, could you explore publishing your work traditionally?

What trends did you see in your ten-book analysis that supports your book? What trends are counter to your book?

If you're planning on traditional publishing, are there any publishers that you can target for your books based on the publishers you noted in your analysis? If you're self-publishing, what trends in cover and content work for your book? If you've already published, is there anything you should change for your current titles and continue to do for future titles?

Once you finish all this research, you may want to review and revise some of your ideas in the rest of the business plan.

Get in the Bag

You want to get your book in the bag/shopping cart of buyers, right? You'll do that with a marketing plan. You'll need few sections to develop your strategies — My Reader, Branding, and Books.

My Reader

Who is your ideal reader? Are they male or female, old or young, educated or not, the CEO of a company or a burger-flipper, a voracious reader or someone who only picks up a book when they have to?

Try writing out a very specific bio of this person. Sure, you'll have readers outside of this demographic, but knowing who that ideal reader is will help you focus your marketing efforts.

Branding

The branding section is all about you. Who are you as an author and what can you do so that people know that. Think of your author persona as you would a book cover. I should be able to tell what kind of author you are from all the places I see and hear about you. A big part of your author branding will be your writing. If you write dark paranormal mysteries, you'll have a very different brand than if you write accounting manuals.

Here's where we talk about building your platform. Yeah, that weird nebulous word that nobody can seem to define. The best explanation I've ever heard is from the book-marketing guru Penny C. Sansevieri.

Definitely check out her books and newsletter for great ideas on marketing yourself and your books. I went to a workshop she presented for my local writers' group, where she taught us this one simple truth:

Platform = Fans

Building your platform is all about getting more fans. Even if you're unpublished, you want to build your fan base for the day your first book comes out. And how does one go about building a platform? Not with a hammer.

The first place to start is with a social media plan. Remember, if social media scares you a whole bunch, I can give you a nice warm introduction in The Coffee Break Guide to Social Media for Writers. The book breaks down what you can do in social media in coffee-break timeframes, so you don't take away from your butt-in-the-chair—writing time.

Here are some things to consider for your platform and brand-building plan:

An author website: I've said it before, and I'll probably say it again. This one is pretty much non-negotiable. You need one. I promise I won't tell you that you have to do anything else, but you have to have a website. You need a home base for your fans and future fans to connect with you and your book.

You can hire someone to design your site, or you can build it yourself (think WordPress), and pay someone to update it someday when you can afford it. Professional web design can mean the difference between selling a few books to your neighbors and friends and actually building a fan base. So you'll need someone to help you with your site eventually. Put it in your plan.

Social media: Don't roll your eyes or run away scared at this point. You can do social media. I promise. If you're not on any social media now, choose one site you're interested in using and start from there. Then put it into your plan to expand from there. Just remember the key to building your online platform is true engagement with real people, and authentic content from you. *The point of social media is to be social, not marketing.*

You might also plan to have someone do graphic design work that you can use on your website and your social media sites. You'll be building your author brand through a consistent look.

It's a good idea to have a consistent author bio to use everywhere online. Write a few that all go together. Write one that is very short, less than 140 characters, to fit on sites like Twitter. Then build on that one to write a medium-sized version. It should be a couple of paragraphs at most to be used for things like PR, speaking engagements, blogs, and on an Amazon author page. Finally, you should use those two bios to develop a slightly longer bio, about four or five paragraphs, that you can use for your publisher and your website.

Don't forget your professional author picture. Let us see that mug of yours everywhere.

Appearances: This is the final bit of building your author brand and platform. Yes, we'd all like a book tour furnished by our publisher, where we are put up at five-star hotels, but that's not actually what I mean here by appearances.

Anyplace where you can talk with people and let them know who you are and what you write, is an appearance, for the purposes of your marketing plan. This can include meetings or conferences of any book, reader, or writer organizations you belong to, workshops you attend or present, and book readings, talks, and signings you have. If you can think of more, great. Add those to your plan too.

The Book Marketing Plan

So you have a book coming out. Yay! How are you going to let people know? The key to marketing is not pushing your book in people's faces (figuratively or literally) but gaining awareness.

Here are a few ideas to consider when working to get that book into people's hands.

When is the book release? How much time do you have to build up awareness before the release day? Can you put together a calendar of when you'll implement different marketing efforts? When, how, and where can you mention on social media how excited you are about the book? Will you do some sort of a virtual release party?

Reviews are king when it comes to word-of-mouth marketing. When will you start sending your book to reviewers? What reviewers will you target? Book bloggers, Amazon power reviewers, newspapers? Don't forget to ask your friends and family for reviews, too. Everyone knows that the first review on any book is probably from your mom and the next two are from your friends, but do you have any writer friends who will give you a good honest review? Just be sure that when you ask for a review, professionally or not, you make the request personalized.

Make sure the people you ask actually read in your genre and remember that they have names and feelings. Addressing a pro reviewer by name will get you a lot closer to obtaining that five-star recommendation than a generic "Dear Reviewer . . . " letter.

Can you do any book giveaways? You can do these on your website, on a blog tour, on social media, or on sites like Goodreads and BookLikes. Don't forget to figure in the cost of books and mailings if you're giving away print copies.

Do you have a newsletter and/or a blog, where you can announce the book release to your biggest fans? This is the place for exclusive content, like cover reveals, extras that you can't get in the book (like short stories or tips and tricks), and any other fun stuff readers might like.

Are there any authors in your genre who you can cross promote with? Don't be afraid to contact them and exchange ideas.

How you use back matter (you know, the stuff after the story in the back of the book) is important, too. Do you have previews and links of your other books? Do you have a letter from you, the author, thanking the readers and asking them for reviews?

A Note on Swag and Ads:

Book marketing is not like trying to sell a car or even a hamburger. We invest a lot of time into reading a book, so whatever you offer to readers has to be worth hours and hours of their precious time. Buying advertisements in magazines, papers, or on radio are expensive, and it's really hard to quantify any results from them. If you do purchase advertising, consider targeting book blogs for your genre, or other websites that target your particular audience.

Too many authors are tempted to buy a bunch of swag items, like bookmarks, postcards, pens, and rulers with the book cover on them. They hand them out at meetings and conferences in hopes that someone will see it and take an interest, enough to actually go out and buy a copy of the book. In reality, most paper items like that go in the trash. Sorry. Swag items are better as a reward for your fans or to give to someone you meet personally and who takes an interest in your work. So be careful spending your money there.

Instead of wasting your money on swag and ads, consider how many books you could afford to give away for the same price. Your actual book is much better advertising than a gimmick. Then ask those people to give honest feedback on how they like the book. Remember, reviews are king. And a recommendation to a friend about a great book is the emperor.

The best marketing for your book is the next one. Don't spend so much time marketing one book that you don't have time to write more.

The Bank

Show me the money! Please?

It's hard to know how much money an average author makes. It's not something you can Google with ease. Well, you can search online for that info pretty easily, but you won't find any really good answers. That's because authors make anywhere from negative income, sleeping on your brother's couch mooching for food, to multi-katrillions.

"They" say that ten percent of people who say they are going to write a book do, and ten percent of that ten percent actually finish it. Ten percent of those finished books will find their way to agents, editors, and self-publishing platforms. Ten percent of those submitted to the gatekeepers will be accepted. Ten percent of all published books will earn out their advance (or the money it took to self-publish the book), and ten percent of those will make a profit.

Are you part of the ten percent?

Just the fact that you're writing your author business plan gets you a lot closer. You're serious about publishing. It's time to run the numbers.

This is the part where a spreadsheet is going to come in handy. I've got one at

www.coffeebreaksocialmedia.com/books/resources that you can download for free to get you started. I recommend a yearly budget that you review at the end of each year and then redo it based on your current situation.

You'll use the other parts of your plan to help you figure out where you'll make and spend your money, so have those sections available. Here are some things to consider when calculating your numbers.

Income

The first thing most authors think of when they are pondering income from writing is the money they get from actually selling the books. But there's a whole lot more to think about.

Traditional print publishing

Advances are a big part of the traditional publishing model (and one that is quickly diminishing and going out of style). Will you get an advance for you book(s)? Maybe. But how much will it be? This is a much harder question to answer. Yes, there are authors who get millions for advances. I truly hope you get to be one of those. But remember that whole ten percent thing? Yeah.

There aren't many resources for finding out how much publishers pay for advances. Here are a couple of suggestions.

If you're part of a writers' group that has published authors, you might bring it up. I'm not saying ask how much someone makes; that's just uncouth and rude. But you might ask some of the published authors if they would be willing to give some general numbers (like a range).

Brenda Hiatt, a successful Romance author, has a bi-annual call for exactly that information. She asks published romance authors to let her know information about how much money they make. She asks for advance numbers, how long it takes to earn out an advance, and continuing royalties for individual publishers based on the information in the contracts. The information is all anonymous and updated continually. It is only based on romance publishers, but if there is no information available for your genre, it's a good starting point. Visit her at brendahiatt.com/show-me-the-money/. And if you happen to be a published romance author, consider sending her your information.

After an advance, you can earn money from selling other rights to your books. Foreign rights are the most common to sell. But there's also money to be made selling movie rights, print rights, digital rights, and more. An agent or a publishing lawyer are the best people to help you understand what these rights are, and how to make money from them.

Once your book is published, you can hopefully look forward to royalties. In traditional publishing, you will need to earn out your advance — if you got one. An advance is money given to you before you earn any profit. It's an advance to you from your future earnings. This means the royalties you would be earning is applied to the amount of the advance. Once all of that money has been earned, you've paid the publisher back for the money they advanced you.

Some publishers will also keep some royalty money in reserve for returns. Books that a bookstore orders to carry on its shelves aren't paid for until after someone actually buys them from the store. They are on loan. If the bookstore doesn't sell as many books as they thought they would, they can return the extras. Usually those books are destroyed. You just might have to pay for that. Check your contract.

If all goes smoothly and you start selling a truckload of books, then you'll earn some royalties. Most larger publishers pay royalties twice a year, approximately four to six months after the end of the reporting period. So an average scenario for earning royalties would look like this:

- Sell the book to a publishing company
- Sign a contract, three to six months later.
- Book goes to print six to twenty-four months later.

- Earn out your advance three months to five years later (and possibly never).
- Receive your first royalty check seven to twelve months after you earned out your advance.

Depending on your publisher, it could take less time, although probably not by much, or it could take much, much, much longer. Depending on how big your advance is and how well your book is selling, you could see royalties nine months after your print date. Or never.

Most traditional print publishers pay around 7–8 percent royalties. This means that if your book sells for $10.00, you'll earn $0.70–0.80 per book. But again, check your contract, because your royalty percentage could vary by several percent, and could be based off net price, (how much the publisher makes on the book) not cover price. A royalty based off net could mean a lot of different things and it may be hard to pin your publisher down to what that actually means.

Traditional e-publishing

Most traditional publishers that print your book in digital format only do not offer any advance. The tradeoff is higher royalty rates, and royalties paid sooner. Royalties for traditional publishers vary from 6 to 40 percent for the most part, with 25 percent being a good average.

Here's a timeline for an average traditional e-published book:

- Sell the book to a publishing company.
- Sign a contract one to three months later.
- Book is digitally published three to six months later.
- Receive your first royalty check two to nine months later.

E-publishing is usually a faster track to getting a royalty check, as you can see. The drawback is not being able to see that book in print, or have your books bought and sold on traditional bookstore shelves.

Most of the larger publishers who buy your book for print are also buying the digital rights, so you would likely have some sort of scenario between these two timelines. Some of the smaller publishers will only print books if you attain a certain amount of sales. Others still only publish digitally, and you may be able to sell your print rights elsewhere, or self-publish print versions of your book for sale.

Self-publishing

One of the advantages of self-publishing is that you can start earning money on your published work faster than with traditional publishing. However, you'll never get an advance in self-publishing (unless you pay it to yourself!). You'll also bear the entire load of the publisher, including the costs.

Here's an average timeline to earning royalties with self-publishing though an e-tailer like Amazon:

- Publish the book.
- Receive your first royalty check from online retailers two month later
- Receive additional royalies owed to you each subsequent month.

Quite a few less steps, huh? But don't forget that there are infinitely more steps in preparing the book for publication. Another advantage to self-publishing is not having to try to interpret a publisher's royalty statement. There are whole classes on how to do that. And they'll make your eyes cross.

The information you'll get from Amazon, etc. is much easier to interpret. It will let you know how many books you have sold, and how much money you made from those sales. If you're selling in both print and digital, there will be two rows of numbers instead of one. Easy peasy.

Another factor you might need to consider for self-publishing is for books you sell yourself. There are new platforms that allow you to set up your own bookstore right on your website so that you can sell your books directly. If you have books in print, you may also have them available for sale at readers' conventions, conferences, and trade shows. It's even really easy to accept credit cards with the Smartphone credit card readers or PayPal.

The extra factor, besides the income, is sales tax. Check with your state and your accountant (which I hope I've convinced you to hire) on the rules and regulations in your area for sales tax.

There are other ways to earn money as a writer than just selling your book, getting an advance, and royalties. Check out the section in chapter three on alternative and passive incomes. But also consider ideas like workshops, mentoring, affiliate work, editing, merchandise, and more. Plan for that additional and passive income that will boost your numbers, so you can start making money before that three-year plan ends.

Expenditures

There are fewer expenditures for a traditionally published author on the outset than a self-published author, but later on those may even out. Why? In three words, marketing and promotions.

For self-published authors

You have to be a publisher and an author. This means you will incur additional expenses. Use your Acknowledgments section of the plan to help you figure out who you'll be paying for these expenditures.

Here are a few items and vendors you may have to pay to get your book ready to go to print:

Editing — This can include everything from paying your beta readers in cookies, to content editing, copy editing, and proofreading.

Formatting — You will need a separate formatted file for each platform on which you intend to publish. You will also need a whole different file to sell your books in print and digitally.

Cover art — Yes, you can judge a book by its cover. EVERYONE does. Make sure you have great cover art. This means that unless you are a graphic artist, you should probably pay someone to design your cover.

ISBN — Depending on how you publish and who you use to purchase an ISBN number from, it could cost anywhere from nothing, to $25 to $150 per book, depending on the service you use. Bowker is the official source for ISBNs in the United States. Canadians are lucky. ISBNs there are free and you can get them from the federal government.

http://www.collectionscanada.gc.ca/ciss-ssci/index-e.html

If your self-published book is also in print, you can get the barcode for the back of the book from Bowker for $25.

Copyright — Self-published or not, you may have to do your own copyright registration. In the US you can file eco-style for just $35 at http://www.copyright.gov/eco/. If you're in Canada, hit up the CIPO at http://www.cipo.ic.gc.ca/.

There may be other vendors who help you with your book, like distributors for example. If you haven't published yet, you will discover these as you go. And if you have, these could change from book to book.

Every author

There are expenses that you will have no matter your route to publishing. Here are some ideas.

Publication and post-publication expenses

Whether you're publishing traditionally or doing it yourself, you'll have expenses after the book comes out for marketing and promotion. The whole chapter prior to this one talks about putting together your plan to get your book "in the bag." Use your *Get the Book in the Bag* plan to plan this part of the budget.

Marketing budget

Consider setting aside a certain amount of your income from each book to go toward marketing the next one, or you can set aside a specific dollar amount you'll spend on each marketing campaign. The reason it is so important to maintain a budget is that it is way too easy to throw money away and then end up with no idea of what worked and what didn't work. There's a place on the book sales tracking sheet to detail your marketing efforts, and if you're self-publishing, side-by-side with your sales numbers. If you don't have access to sales information I recommend your sales rank. This way you can get a good idea of what does actually have an effect. Download the spreadsheet for free at

www.CoffeeBreakSocialMedia.com/Books/Resources.

It's a good idea to use your production schedule to help plan your marketing schedule. It doesn't matter if you're doing book giveaways, blog tours, going to reader conventions, or buying ads on Goodreads and Facebook, you'll spend most of your money just before and after a release. Be sure you know when you are going to spend that money so that there aren't any surprises.

Another part of your marketing and promotions plan, and your budget, is your ongoing branding. Remember to include the cost of your website (like hosting fees, domain registration, and any graphic design you commission) and any other annual or regular payments for the upkeep of your name.

Professional development

You're doing everything you can to be the best author you can. You read lots of books, take classes, join professional organizations, and go to conferences. You budget for the money you're going to spend on all of those smart moves. Use your goals and your Acknowledgements plan to help you decide how much money you can spend on becoming a better author.

Office supplies

We all need paper and pens. Computers are good, too. I once went crazy and spent $300 dollars at Office Depot. On what? I'm not sure. Do as I say and not as I did. Be realistic about what kinds of office supplies you need. Remember to include assets like a new computer or a desk when you think you truly need them.

Professional services

Do you have an agent, lawyer, accountant, or assistant? This is the place to run the numbers on what you can afford to pay them. Use your *Acknowledgments* plan to help you see what money you may spend on these services.

CHAPTER 8

Book By Book

So you want to write a mini-business plan for an individual book. Okay. I've broken this up into seven parts similar to those of your author plan, but more suited to an individual project.

Project Summary

State the genre of your book, your word count (or estimated word count), the theme and the logline for your book.

The logline is the high concept. You have one sentence to describe what your book is about. This is also known as the "elevator pitch." If you need help understanding and writing your logline, movies are a great place to start.

Here's an example: A respected paleontologist visits an island amusement park where real dinosaurs roam, but chaos reigns and he must save not only himself, but two children and a handful of other people from being eaten.

What movie? Yep, you guessed it. Jurassic Park.

Can you write something like that for your book? I know it's hard to wop 100,000 words down to one sentence, but if you can do that, you've got yourself a great high-concept story with some serious sale-ability. (Yes, that's a real word. Even if I (might have) made it up.)

If you need more help with loglines, I recommend Alexandra Sokoloff's website, www.screenwritingtricks.com. She has several posts on premise and high concept that will really help.

Once you have your logline, you might want to write a summary or a synopsis of the story. Synopsis is a dreaded word among authors. If it makes you break out in hives, don't do it. Just write a short summary of the story, or items you will cover in a non-fiction book. You can write the synopsis even if you haven't written the book (and if you are submitting a proposal, you'll probably have to). You can always change and update your synopsis when you've finished. They seem to be so much harder to write than the book itself. Here are a couple of tricks to help you:

Start with your back cover blurb. This is two, maybe three paragraphs, hitting the highlights of the book, minus the ending. Read the cover blurbs of some of your favorite books and emulate those. You can also go chapter by chapter, but limit yourself to a couple of sentences about what happens, or what you talk about in each chapter.

For fiction

Plot points can be a great way to keep your synopsis focused. Go beyond the three-act structure here. If you've studied story structure, go back and review the parts. Use each of them to write a paragraph for your short synopsis. If you need more resources, some of my favorites are Dan Wells 7 Plot Points, Michael Hauge's Six Stages, and the Hero's Journey.

For non-fiction

If your book is a guide, how-to, or manual, include information like who this will help, how it's different from other non-fiction books, and give some bulleted points. If it's a report, biography/memoir, or the like, you can give highlights similar to plot points in a fiction book.

Production schedule

You'll need to develop a schedule for your book. Start with a writing schedule. I personally like tracking how many words I write each day. Once you have your writing schedule set, there are other developmental timelines to consider.

Editing can involve many facets. This includes your own edits of your first draft, working with your critique partners, beta readers, copy edits, and proofreading. Don't forget to work in time for your revisions.

If your path is traditional publishing, you might include timelines for sending out queries, waiting for rejections, and conversations with agents and editors who are interested in your work.

If your path is self-publishing, you'll need schedules for production and publication tasks, besides editing, like cover art, formatting, uploading the book, and the wait time until your book is uploaded to the various resellers.

Competitive Analysis

Are there any other books out there similar to yours? Who else writes books in your genre? Are there any other books with your title? Start with these three questions and brainstorm who and what your book will be competing against for sales. If you answers are no, nope, and of course not, that's not necessarily a good thing. Yes, we hope to write something unique, but be careful of being so outside of the box that you don't actually have an audience. Use the same questions (or the worksheet available on the Coffee Break website) to get a clear picture of the competition for this book.

Once you know who your competition is, you can get a good idea of who your ideal reader is. Use that information to focus your marketing efforts.

Marketing

Think about having a calendar (maybe side-by-side with your production/writing schedule) for your marketing efforts. Know when and what kind of marketing you'll do, including social media. Having that calendar will help you make the most of your efforts and prevent you from wasting money and the time you could spend writing. Knowing well in advance what kind of marketing you do for your book will make it less stressful.

Regardless of your chosen path to publication, you'll need a marketing plan. Consider three separate timeframes: pre-release, release, and post-release.

If you are an unpublished or pre-published author, a big part of your pre-release marketing is building your platform and making connections. It's never too soon to start. In fact, I think the moment you decide to write professionally you should start. That way you'll be years ahead of the authors who start when they sign their first contract or publish themselves. But if you are one of those people, it's okay. Get to building now. You'll have to put a bit more time and effort into this part of your plan, but it's totally doable.

A big part of building your platform is having a website and being active on social media. Decide what social media sites you're either already familiar with, or think are important, and plan into your timeline how long you'll be spending on those sites.

If you're already published, you still need to spend some time building and maintaining your current platform, but you'll also want to think about the build up to this book's release. Can you do cover reveals, excerpts on your blog, or contact local writers' groups and bookstores to do a book talk? Why, yes, you can do all of these things!

Release day is exciting. For your schedule, make sure you don't overbook yourself the week before, the day of, or the week after. You'll have plenty to do. Trust me. Think about the time it will take to schedule a blog tour (unless your publisher does that for you, or you hire a marketing company to arrange it. There are a lot of companies out there now that can put together a blog tour for you relatively inexpensively, anything from $25 to $1,000.)

Distribution Plan

If you're self-published, you need to think about how you are going to actually get books into people's hands or e-readers. E-pubbing on Amazon is the logical place to start, but where else can you have your books for sale?

CHAPTER 9

Tracking and Evaluating Your Business Plan

Tracking

You put a whole lot of time and effort into planning your business. Make sure you're tracking your progress. How? Here are a few ideas:

- Keep a checklist of your goals. When you accomplish one, check it off.
- Keep a calendar for your production and marketing schedule. Check off when you get those tasks accomplished.
- Update your budget when you spend or make money.
- There are free downloadable worksheets for all of these at www.CoffeeBreakSocialMedia.com/Books/Resources.

Tools To Track Progress

Amazon Author Central

If your books are for sale on Amazon, you have an author central page. It's mega-useful. One of the fun tools available there is the BookScan information for you book. Lookie there. How many books you sold and when. Make a note of when you do your marketing efforts and how your sales are affected in the following time frames.

Google Analytics

You can add analytics to any website you own that will help you track who, what, when, where, why, and from where your website visitors are viewing your page. Facebook has some similar analytics/insights for fan pages.

Klout

Want to see how your social media efforts are panning out? Plug yourself into Klout and see how your score increases or decreases over time.

Evaluation

Phew! So you wrote a business plan and you went forth into the world, plan in hand, to publish your writing. Good job. But how did that year go? It's time to find out.

You need to decide how often you'll revisit your plan and reformulate. Some people like quarterly reviews, some bi-annually, some yearly, and others would prefer to never look at the plan again. I recommend somewhere between every few months and once a year. Try going through your plan section by section and taking a look at what worked, what didn't, and what needs to change. You can download the worksheet for this evaluation at

www.CoffeeBreakSocialMedia.com/Books/Resources.

Goals

- Look through your goals for this year. Which ones did you meet? Which ones didn't you meet? Why?
- What strategies that you used actually advanced your goals, and which ones didn't do squat?
- Now check out your future goals. Are they still the same? What's changed? (They will change, as you gain more knowledge and the publishing landscape changes.)
- What goals do you want to accomplish in the upcoming year?

Blurb & Cover

- Has your reason for writing changed? How and why does that affect your goals for the coming years?
- Are you still writing in the same genre? Have you added new areas to write in?

- How has your publishing model worked for you this year? Is it time to focus that or expand it?
- Have there been game-changing developments in the landscape of publishing that you need to take into consideration?
- How much did you write this year, and/or how many books did you publish?
- How much money have you made from publishing? How much did you spend on your publishing efforts? Do either of those numbers need to change?
- Did you receive any accolades for your work? How did that help or hinder you?
- Who are you writing for? Has that changed?
- Were your education and qualifications sufficient enough to aid you in your efforts this year? Do you need to do something different for the next year, to get the information you need to be successful?
- Does your Muse Statement still resonate with you? Are there any changes to it you could make to really give it some oomph?
- Did you encounter any of the obstacles you planned for or did you need to use any of your contingency plans? How did those work out for you?
- Are you happy with what you did over the last year? Are you happy with your choices and what you're doing? What needs to change?

Acknowledgements

- Who in your publishing team really worked well for you, and who needs the boot?
- Is there anyone you need to add to your team? How and where will you find that key person?

The Chapters

- How did your writing process work for you this year? Did you have to make any adjustments to the way you write a book? Why and how?
- How much did you actually produce this year? Did you meet your goals? Why or why not?
- How did your deadlines work for you? Were you able to make them or do you need to make realistic adjustments?
- How were your stress levels about your production schedule? Do they need adjustment because of levels of stress, or do you think you could do more?
- Did you get through the items you needed on your Author Entrepreneur checklist? Is there anything you need to add?

The Shelues

- What's the new buzz in the publishing industry this year and how does that affect you?
- Are the books and authors you identified on Your Shelf still viable competition? Has anything interesting happened with those books, authors, or publishers this year?

Get In The Bag

- How is your author branding? Did your efforts gain you more awareness by readers?
- Did you accomplish your social media plan efforts? Is it time to step it up to the next level or are you spending too much time phaffing about on Facebook?
- How much money did you spend on marketing your book? Did it pay off? How do you know?
- Are there any other marketing efforts you'd like to try this year?

Rewards

An important part of evaluation is rewarding yourself for the goals you did accomplish. Make sure you celebrate your successes. You can give yourself a gold star and hang your business plan on the refrigerator for the whole family to see, or go big and take a vacation. Viva Las Vegas
!

CHAPTER 10

See, You Can Do This

Well Done

I love being a writer, but let's face it, it's not exactly an easy business. I bet you've seen those picture montages that show "What my mom thinks I do" with a picture of a writer dancing around with some imaginary friends, then "What my friends think I do" with the picture of an author faceplanted on a keyboard sleeping, with drool coming out of their mouth, then, "What the world thinks I do" with a picture of Richard Castle on book tour and finally "What I actually do" with a picture of a writer slaving over a laptop, fingers bleeding.

It's so true. Only other writers truly get what we all do every day. The author entrepreneur isn't some pansy. The publishing industry is complex and convoluted on its good days. So I say, well done for taking on this business on. And by working your way through this book, you've taken control of your writing career.

My hope is that with the ideas and steps in this book you'll get closer to realizing your own career dreams. Dream big, and with your shiny new plan in hand go out there and be the writer you really want to be!

Resources

Templates

If you missed any of the resources listed throughout the book you can go to www.coffeebreaksocialmedia.com/books/resources to download the worksheets or templates. Most are available for Word, Excel or PDF.

Here is a list of what's available:

- The Business Plan template
- The ten-question Coffee Break Business plan template
- Book by Book Business Plan template
- Goals template
- Yearly Evaluation
- Your Bookshelf Competitive Analysis
- Query Submissions Tracker
- Sales and Rankings Tracker
- Budget template

Websites

I also mentioned quite a few websites that I found useful. For hyperlinks go to my website www.coffeebreaksocialmedia.com Here are URLs for those:

Coffee Break Social Media – www.coffeebreaksocialmedia.com

Amazon's Author Central – https://authorcentral.amazon.com

CreateSpace :Amazon's self-publishing arm – www.createspace.com

Smashwords: Another self-publishing website and bookstore – www.smashwords.com

Lulu: Another self-publishing website and bookstore – www.lulu.com/publish

Romance Writers of America – www.rwa.org

Sisters in Crime – www.sistersincrime.org

Science Fiction and Fantasy Writers of America – www.sfwa.org

American Society of Journalists and Authors – www.asja.org
Society of Children's Book Writers and Illustrators – www.scbwi.org

The Internal Revenue Service's page about business or hobby - http://www.irs.gov/uac/Business-or-Hobby%3F-Answer-Has-Implications-for-Deductions

The Amazon associate/affiliate information page – https://affilliate-program.amazon.com

Zazzle: an online merchandising tool – www.zazzle.com/sell

CafePress: another online merchandising tool – http://www.cafepress.com/cp/shopkeepers/index.aspx?page=make-money

Apache's Open Office – www.openoffice.org

Libre Office – www.libreoffice.org

KOffice - http://www.kde.org/applications/office/

NeoOffice – www.neooffice.org

Calibre: an e-book organization and creation tool - http://calibre-ebook.com/

Scrivener: writing and e-book creation software - http://www.literatureandlatte.com

StoryToolz: has great tools for tracking wordcount – www.storytoolz.com

Kindle Cloud Reader - https://read.amazon.com/

Goodreads giveaways – https://www.goodreads.com/giveaway/new

Booklikes giveaways - http://booklikes.com/giveaways

Bowker: the US seller of ISBNs –
https://www.myidentifiers.com/isbn/main

CISS: the Canadian keepers of the ISBNs –
http://www.collectionscanada.gc.ca/ciss-ssci/index-e.html

Google Analytics - http://www.google.com/analytics/

Klout: a website for measuring your social media effectiveness
An interactive tool on understanding the – www.klout.com

Hero's Journey: An interactive video that explains this archetype
http://www.readwritethink.org/files/resources/interactives/herosjourne
y/

Writing Gurus

Penny C. Sansevieri's Author Marketing Experts website –
http://www.amarketingexpert.com/

Alexandra Sokoloff's blog – www.screenwritingtips.com

Dan Well's videos on the seven plot points of story structure –
http://youtu.be/KcmiqQ9NpPE

Michael Hauge's Six Stages –
http://www.storymastery.com/articles/30-screenplay-structure

Brenda Hiatt's Show Me The Money report –
http://brendahiatt.com/show-me-the-money/

Books

There are also a bunch of books I recommended that you might find useful too.:

The Secret by Ronda Byrne

The Right Brain Business Plan by Jennifer Lee

The Coffee Break Guide to Social Media for Writers by Amy Denim

The Coffee Break Guide to Author Websites by Diane Whiddon

The Coffee Break Guide to Social Media for Writers

HOW TO SUCCEED ON SOCIAL MEDIA AND STILL HAVE TIME TO WRITE

CHAPTER 1

The Social Media Monster

Don't Let Social Media Scare You

When I first got serious about writing, I joined a local writing group. Best idea I ever had. They've given me so much support from day one. I highly recommend this step for anyone who wants to make a go at writing and selling his or her work.

One of the first events my group put on after I joined was a writers' retreat. We went up to the mountains, got all inspired by the wildlife, the scenery, and the hot tub. There may also have been some wine involved. Good times.

We spent a chunk of the weekend putting words on the page. But, we also had a few guest speakers to boost our morale and inspire our writing. One of our presenters was an editor from a small, but growing, press. Her topic was query letters, but as writers and editors tend to do, we moved off like a rocket on a tangent.

Social media.

And it scared the living nightlife out of me.

She threw around words like platform, followers, tweet, and discoverability. This big bad scary editor said I should have my platform established two years before I submitted anything. Ahhhh!

I didn't even know what a platform was, much less how to create one online. I wasn't on Twitter, I'd never heard of Goodreads, Pinterest was just a funny word, and the only time I spent on Facebook was to take weird surveys, play farming games, and tag pictures of my drunken friends.

But, if I wanted to be a published author, it seemed I needed to do more than just write. Who knew?

This relaxing weekend in the mountains left me in need of some meditation and a massage. But I skipped the yoga and went out and bought a smartphone instead.

I spent the next year becoming a social media fiend. And I barely finished one manuscript. I had created an online presence, but I had diddly-squat to pitch. Oops.

The purpose of writing this book is, A. To help all those authors out there who've been scared by social media create their own online platform, and 2. Give them time to actually write.

Novel concept. I know.

Social media doesn't have to be scary. You can use social media effectively (it's really not as scary as some people I know make it out to be) and still have time to write. Social media can be your friend. I'll get you an introduction.

Author, this is Social Media. No, wait come back here. I promise it's not the big, scary, mean, time-sucking monster it looks like. Breathe. Okay, good. Let's try again. Author, this is Social Media. Yes, you can shake hands, it won't bite.

Good job.

Social Media, this is Author. You're going to become good friends.

Any time this all becomes too much, come back to this page, breathe, and read the tips again.

Social media is your friend. It doesn't have to take away from the time you spend doing what you love. Five quality minutes a day is all you really need. Thirty quality minutes spread throughout the day will do wonders.

Coffee Break Social Media Tips

- Be present. Don't post and run. Do take on social media when you will be available to interact should someone respond to you—on any of your platforms. The key is to be social and interactive. Not a robot.
- Use a ten-to-one ratio for marketing yourself or your books. For every ten social interactions you can have one, just one self-promo. People don't like, or buy spam.
- As you get into your platforms and your breaks, you'll learn what you do and don't like to do. DO what you like.
- Don't let social media overwhelm you. If you're jumping between platforms and spending more time on social media than on what you love to do, scale it back. Start back at the beginning and just concentrate on your primary platform. Ease yourself into other platforms when you are good and ready.

The Best Platform is the Next Book

You can spend all day, every day building your platform on social media, but if you don't actually write a book, it won't do you a bit of good. Establishing your platform and using social media is always time spent not writing your book. Without a book, there's nothing for you to establish a platform for. So, get your butt in the chair and write that book. And when you finish that one, write the next one, and the next one. A good quality story will sell you, your brand, and your books better than any website, Facebook post, or tweet.

How This Book Works

In the next chapter, I'll introduce you to the Coffee Break Mentality. It's the key. Social media is there to give you a boost, but it shouldn't take away from your writing time. The coffee break strategies in this book should help you figure out how to be on social media and still have time to write.

You don't have to read every chapter. After you get those key concepts, you can flip through the next few chapters to check out the writer's best social media sites. There's a chapter on your website and blogging, Facebook, Twitter, Pinterest, and Goodreads. For each, there are details on what you need to do once, every once in a while, what to do once you've got your groove on, and what to do on your social media breaks.

There are so many great social media networks these days, that this would be a four-billion-page book if there were a chapter on each of them. Instead, included is a chapter with twelve additional networks with briefs on how to use them. There is also a chapter on Social Media tools, websites, and services to help you get the most out of your social media efforts.

At the end of the book there is an example social media plan, and templates for you to create your own social media plan.

In case I go too techy-fancy-schmancy on you, there is a glossary at the end of the book where you can get simply worded definitions for some of the terms I use.

For example: Platform — noun, a place where you represent yourself and your writing to the world in order to gain more fans. Examples: your website, your Facebook page, your Twitter account, personal appearances, your books, etc.

One Teeny Tiny Final Note

This book will be out of date the moment it's published. It's simply the nature of social media (or today's world, really). This book will have to be updated, and I'll do that, as well as post updates on my website www.coffeebreaksocialmedia.com. But know going in that something in these pages will be wrong, out of date, or simply not exist anymore when you read this. You'll have to do some research on your own sometimes. It's okay. Google will help you.

Let's get started.

Glossary of Social Media Terms

Amazon - noun, 1. An online retailer of goods, including books. 2. The number one seller of books anywhere in the world.

Amazon affiliate – noun, a person who earns money from referring customers to Amazon when they purchase items from Amazon.

Blog (also see **Vlog**) – noun, an online diary. An online place where you let your fans know what's going on in your world.

Coffee Break Mentality – noun, the idea that you don't have to be on social media for long periods of time but can still be engaging, present, and successful at building your online presence while still having time to write.

Co-op money – money paid by a publisher to retailers for prime positioning within the bookstore/book kiosk (like at airports). This is especially for end cap placement, featured books, special displays, and front-facing books.

Download – verb, to take a picture or video from the Internet and put it on your computer.

Email – noun, a form of communication that uses writing and transmitting via the Internet. Verb — emailing

Facebook – noun, a very popular social networking website where you post updates, pictures, videos, and information about you and your books. Verb, to contact someone via the Facebook website or to spend time perusing and posting to the Facebook website.

Flickr – noun, a website and social network based on sharing pictures and images.

Foursquare – noun, a social network based in checking in at places you visit.

GetGlue – noun, a social network based on watching and talking about TV shows and movies.

Goodreads – noun, a social network for people who love books and reading.

Google – noun, 1. An online search engine. 2. A large company that controls a lot of the Internet business in the world. Verb, to Google, to search for information online.

Google+ - noun, a social network owned and operated by Google where users post updates, pictures, videos, links, and more.

Hashtag – noun, the # symbol. Used on social media networks for denoting keywords, to note that your post relates to a specific conversation, or to note that something is significant or funny, or to express a thought. Words following a hashtag are run together and have no punctuation.

Host – noun, a company that uses its computers and servers to make your website available on the Internet. Verb, to have a company use its computers and servers to make your website available on the internet.

Instagram – noun, a website and social network based on sharing photos.

Last FM – noun, a website and social network based on listening and enjoying music.

Link – a URL/ web address for a website. Usually starts with www. Verb, to make social media networks work together so a post on one also shows up on the others.

LinkedIn – noun, a professional social network.

Loops – noun, an online or email forum where users share information with a specific group.

Mail Chimp – noun, a website that helps you create and send newsletters.

MySpace – noun, a social network that died in the 2000s but was then revived and re-invented by Justin Timberlake as a social network for music.

Network – noun, a place on the Internet where you make connections with other people.

Verb – to make connections with people.

Newsletter – noun, a short publication used to send information to and update subscribers on an author's new releases and appearances.

Pin – verb, to share a picture or video on Pinterest.

Noun, the actual picture or video shared on Pinterest.

Pinterest – noun, a website and social media network based on sharing pictures and videos.

Platform – noun, 1. A social media website you socialize on, brand yourself, and let people know about you and your writing. Examples: website, blog, Facebook, Twitter. 2. The information you put out about you and your writing that brands you. Example: A Facebook post with a hot-looking cowboy, a tweet about macaroni and cheese, a blog post about one's favorite iPhone apps.

Plug-in – noun, a tool used on websites like Wordpress to add content or make the site easier to use.

Post – verb, to put content like pictures, videos, writing, etc. on your blog, website, or social network.

Noun, the actual content you have put on your blog, website, or social media network.

Profile – noun, information about you. This usually includes a picture and a short bio.

Retweet – verb, to send a tweet from another user to all of your followers on Twitter. Related: ReVine and RePin.

SEO – noun, an acronym standing for Search Engine Optimization. The concept of using keywords to make your website or content easier to find by search engines such as Google and Bing.

Social media – noun, Internet-based communities where people can interact, post information, pictures, and more. Aka: Your friend. Examples: Facebook, Twitter.

Social Media Barista – noun, a person who is the master of a particular social media network and is ready to do advanced techniques.

Social Media Coffee Breaks (SMCBs) - noun, short five- to fifteen-minute breaks in your writing that you use to be present and engaging on social media.

Social Media Tool – noun, a website or application that helps you be more effective on social media.

Spotify - noun, a website and social network based on listening and enjoying music.

Tribe – noun, a group of users that have joined together for the purpose of sharing each other's blog posts using Triberr.

Triberr – noun, a website for bloggers where they can share content with other members and have their content shared by other members.

Tumblr – noun, a website that is a cross between a blogging site and a social network.

Tweet – verb, to post a message, picture, video, or link on Twitter.

Twitter – noun, an online social network where people communicate using 140 characters or less. Verb, to tweet

Upload – verb, posting things like pictures or videos to a website. Usually requires an extra step and a tool on the website to do it.

Vine – noun, an application that hosts short six-second videos that users produce and upload.

Vlog – noun, a video blog.

Website – noun, 1. That place on the Internet that you call home. 2. The home base to where all of your social media is linked. 3. The place where your fans find all the latest and greatest information about you.

Widget - noun, a tool used on websites like Wordpress to add content, sometimes directly from another website.

Wordpress.com– noun, a website that allows its users to create their own websites and blogs.

Wordpress.org – noun, a website that allows its users to create their own websites and blog using their own URL.

Yahoo! – noun, an Internet company that provides services like email and loops.

YouTube – noun, a website and search engine that hosts videos mostly created by the users.

Your People – noun, the people on social networks that are like-minded to you. They may be fans, writers, friends, family, or other supporters of you and your work.

If you enjoyed this excerpt and would like more help succeeding on social media, but still have time to write the book is available for Kindle or in paperback. Go to http://amzn.to/1cA1tBF to buy it now.

A Thank You
From the Author

Dear Reader (who is probably also a writer),
Before you are off to read your next book I wanted to take a quick moment to say thank you for reading this one.

When you go shopping for books to help improve your writing life they are often on the writing craft, but you chose another direction and took a chance on learning about business plans with me. I appreciate that you downloaded and read this book all the way to the end (where you are now).

Remember there are a lot of great free downloadable resources just for readers of this book. If you missed clicking on the links in any chapter, the templates can all be accessed at
www.coffeebreaksocialmedia.com/books/resources.

We all know reviews are the king of word-of-mouth marketing. I would be eternally grateful if you would spread the word about The Coffee Break Guide to Business Plans for Writers. It will help me understand what you liked, what was useful, and to write more business books for authors like you.

Would you take a minute to leave a review for this book on Amazon?

When you review on Amazon, they give you the chance to rate the book and share it on Facebook and Twitter. If your writer friends out there in the social-media-o-sphere might like (or need) this book to help them focus their writing life like you have, please let them know about it. You can get me at:

@AmyDenim on Twitter

Facebook: www.facebook.com/AuthorAmyDenim

If you liked the content and found the information here useful please let me know. If you have corrections or suggestions for the next version, get those to me too. I love to hear from readers and writers.

Best wishes,

~Amy

ABOUT THE AUTHOR

Amy Denim writes business books for writers and contemporary romance. She loves hot heroes (like chefs and cowboys) and curvy intelligent heroines (like chefs and cowgirls.)

She's been a franchise sales coordinator, a lifeguard, a personal shopper, and a teacher of English as a Foreign Language. But now she spends her days reading and writing at her local library or in her book cave.

Amy started out her writer's life scared out of her wits because she didn't have a business plan, hadn't yet created an online platform, wasn't on twitter, didn't have a Facebook fanpage and had never even heard of Goodreads. She just wrote books. So she spent a year becoming a publishing industry information fiend and now does consulting for creatives on how to use take control of their writing careers. She started Coffee Break Social Media to help writers and artists learn to use SM platforms effectively (without the scare tactics) but still have time to create. She believes business plans and social media can be every writer's friend, sometimes they just need an introduction.

Visit Amy on her author website at www.AmyDenim.com or for tips and tricks on the writing business at www.coffeebreaksocialmedia.com.